Higher Education Planning in an Exponential Age

Higher Education Planning in an Exponential Age

A Continuous, Dynamic Process

Darrel W. Staat

ROWMAN & LITTLEFIELD
Lanham • Boulder • New York • London

Published by Rowman & Littlefield
An imprint of The Rowman & Littlefield Publishing Group, Inc.
4501 Forbes Boulevard, Suite 200, Lanham, Maryland 20706
www.rowman.com

6 Tinworth Street, London SE11 5AL, United Kingdom

Copyright © 2021 by Darrel W. Staat

All rights reserved. No part of this book may be reproduced in any form or by any electronic or mechanical means, including information storage and retrieval systems, without written permission from the publisher, except by a reviewer who may quote passages in a review.

British Library Cataloguing in Publication Information Available

Library of Congress Cataloging-in-Publication Data

Names: Staat, Darrel W., 1941– author. | American Association of Community Colleges, issuing body.
Title: Higher education planning in an exponential age : a continuous, dynamic process / Darrel W. Staat.
Description: Lanham : Rowman & Littlefield, [2021] | "Published in cooperation with the American Association of Community Colleges." | Includes bibliographical references. | Summary: "This book fulfills a need for planning in higher education due to the impending impact of ten twenty-first century technologies: 3D printing, artificial intelligence, autonomous vehicles, bitcoin/blockchain, genome development: agricultural, genome: medical, internet of things, nanotechnology, personal robots, and quantum computing" — Provided by publisher.
Identifiers: LCCN 2020058091 (print) | LCCN 2020058092 (ebook) | ISBN 9781475859683 (cloth) | ISBN 9781475859690 (paperback) | ISBN 9781475859706 (ebook)
Subjects: LCSH: Education, Higher—Effect of technological innovations On—United States. | Educational planning—United States. | Universities and colleges—United States—Administration. | Education, Higher—Research—United States. | Education, Higher—Aims and Objectives—United States.
Classification: LCC LB2395.7 .S762 2021 (print) | LCC LB2395.7 (ebook) | DDC 378.1/7344678—dc23
LC record available at https://lccn.loc.gov/2020058091
LC ebook record available at https://lccn.loc.gov/2020058092

Contents

Preface	vii
Acknowledgments	xi
Introduction	xiii
1 Toboggan Theory	1
2 Higher Education at the Precipice	7
3 Technological Impact on Higher Education	35
4 Mission and Vision	53
5 ARPAC: A Strategic Planning Process	59
6 ARPAC Step 1: Awareness	65
7 ARPAC Step 2: Research	71
8 ARPAC Step 3: Planning	83
9 ARPAC Step 4: Action	89
10 ARPAC Step 5: Caring	93
11 Toward a Successful Future	97
Epilogue	101
Appendix: The ARPAC Planning Process: Awareness	103

References	111
About the Author	113

Preface

The twenty-first century, with its multiple technologies developing exponentially, creates serious disruptions for the business community and higher education. Although new technologies have been around for centuries, they have always developed in a linear manner, one day at a time, one year to the next, in a logical, step-by-step manner. Primitive bows and arrows over time became the longbow with its tremendous power. Fireworks for entertainment in China developed into cannons with amazing firepower in Europe. Elephants used by Hannibal in the wars with the Romans became tanks in World War I.

The twentieth century saw horseless carriages powered by small gasoline engines become NASCAR racing machines with phenomenal speed. The Wright brothers' success with an engine powered a bi-winged flying machine developed over a series of decades to jet powered airliners, bombers, and fighters. These technologies, plus many more, developed over extended periods of time. They did not jump onto the scene in short order.

The twenty-first century is different. The world has moved rapidly from an industrial age to a digital era. Manufacturing, which had been the bedrock of the twentieth-century economy, was sidestepped in the early twenty-first. There was limited warning of what was happening and little caution of potential disruptions that would impact life and culture. One only has to become aware of Uber, the company that upended the taxi industry, Airbnb which impacted the hotel industry, or Amazon, which disrupted retail business, to see the exponential change.

All three of them seemed to happen overnight, with very little warning. Today, the world is faced with the development of autonomous cars, 3D printing, the Internet of Things, personal robots, medical genome, agricultural genome, Bitcoin/Blockchain, artificial intelligence, nanotechnology, and quantum computing, all of which are developing in a two-stage manner: Stage 1, linear, the one that worked so well for the past century, and Stage 2, exponential, with a velocity that suddenly presents the world with phenomenal, serial disruptions.

The business community is very much aware of what is happening. Those involved with business and industry are racing to learn how the twenty-first-century technologies are going to affect them. They need to understand the impending impacts and learn how to deal with them if they want to survive and prosper in the rapid world of change. It is a matter of learning, adapting to the new successfully, or facing bankruptcy; it is almost that simple.

One important component of the twenty-first-century business will be the need for a significant change in strategic planning. What worked well in the twentieth century is a death knell in the current century. Learning to deal successfully with high velocity changes on a number of fronts is critically important to success when making plans for the future. Those leading the business world know they must prepare for and adapt to what is coming.

This book, however, is not about how to support the business community make its way successfully through the twenty-first century. Rather, it is making an attempt to assist higher education as it, too, moves into a new world of technologies that will develop at breakneck speeds. If institutions of higher education from community colleges to universities continue to operate as they did successfully in the past century, they are headed for certain disaster. Higher education, like the business and industry, will need to make serious changes in the way its leaders think, its faculty teaches, and its students learn.

The purpose of this book is to assist leaders, faculty, and boards in higher education to understand what will soon impact them and how to lead the changes in operation needed for success. Leaders and faculty in higher education must also become futurists, innovators, explainers of the disruptions, and humanitarians. In simple terms, if educators in higher education do not learn to deal with the technologies, the technologies will deal with them.

In order to successfully assist students understand the future they are facing, leaders and faculty in higher education have no choice but learn and show students how to adapt to their future lives and careers. At the core of making the future a success for all concerned is how planning is conducted in this century. This book provides the background needed and a planning process that has the potential to lead to success.

Acknowledgments

I would like to thank Dr. Travis Teague, vice provost and dean at Wingate University, for his assistance and encouragement writing this book. His solid, unflappable leadership in a time of change for the graduate education program is greatly appreciated by all concerned.

Next, I would like to express my sincere appreciation to Dr. Charlesa Hann, assistant dean of graduate education, who has led the department with a steady hand through rough water, which was a great benefit to the faculty, staff, and students. She too has encouraged me in the writing of this book.

As I work in my home office hours on end, I am supported by my dear wife Beverly. I appreciate her efforts on my behalf very much. She is my angel.

Introduction

It is time for another book on planning because of the impending impact of twenty-first-century technologies. Right into the beginning of the twenty-first century, the long shadow of Robert McNamara continued to fall on the thinking of how planning in government, business, and higher education should be developed. His was a logical, step-by-step process that supported looking ahead within set parameters. It focused on the control of variables in a closed system where the manufacturer had everything from raw materials to the finished product under one roof. The process, with many tweaks over the years, worked quite well in the past.

LINEAR DEVELOPMENT

What made it successful was that technologies were developing in a linear manner. One could observe the entire process from a high point in a manufacturing facility. Deciding to improve the product, increase or decrease the deliverables, or financially determining the cost-benefit ratio was relatively easy as there were few disruptions along the way. Those that did rear their heads were taken care of with dispatch. Since the process worked reasonably well, it continued to guide businesses and other organizations for decades.

EXPONENTIAL DEVELOPMENT

In the 1990s the Internet was made available to the public. The digital world, which already existed to a considerable extent, was pushed with great speed into the life of anyone or any business with a computer. In the business world things changed things radically. Businesses large and small developed websites that provided data literally at one's fingertips. Previously, one could only access that information by entering a store or spending time in the library. Almost immediately, a large business in a metropolitan area or a mom-and-pop business in a rural area could use the Internet for marketing and sales. In the late 1990s, all kinds of dot-coms blossomed as the new century approached, some were successful, and most were not. However, their very presence demonstrated that the digital age had taken hold and was not going away.

By 2020, there had been lots of experience with what happens when things go digital. Companies like Intel had created a chip the size of a fingernail with 100 billion transistors. Smart phones had tremendous computer power, much more than it took to place a man to the moon in 1969. Although individuals could stand back and decide against using the digital marvels that existed, the millennial generation and many others, did not. They welcomed it, used it, and adapted to it.

BUSINESS IN THE TWENTY-FIRST CENTURY

The business community followed suit doing everything it could to use and adapt to the digital age. Business leaders had no choice as new technologies developed exponentially and in order to compete in their part of the business world, they had to keep up. If they did not, they were soon threatened with extinction by the competition. Amazon, using the benefits of the digital age, soon found itself in successful competition with retail establishments that had existed for decades or more. Uber and Airbnb staged upsets in the transportation and room service fields. Businesses got the picture; they had to get savvy with the digital exponential age, or lose out.

HIGHER EDUCATION IN THE EARLY TWENTY-FIRST CENTURY

Higher education, however, has moved into the twenty-first century making few changes to its teaching/learning process. Worse yet, it mostly continues to do its planning with the well-worn twentieth-century methods. McNamara's shadow still hangs long. The twentieth-century model continues to work generally because most of higher education from community colleges to universities still have all the variables under one roof. They are able to make decisions on their future directions in much the same way they have for decades. They tend to ignore what is affecting the business community and they continue to exist in an ivory tower.

TEN TECHNOLOGIES

The ten technologies listed in the preface, autonomous cars, 3D printing, the Internet of Things, personal robots, medical genome, agricultural genome, Bitcoin/Blockchain, artificial intelligence, nanotechnology, and quantum computing, are developing differently. Examples of the change can be seen in the development of Uber, Airbnb, and Amazon. In addition to affecting the business community, many of these ten technologies will have a direct impact on the community college and university. It is critical to the future success of higher education that its leaders, faculty, and staff understand what is developing technologically that can impact higher education institutions.

THE TWO STAGES

To deal with the technologies when they move from Stage 1, linear development, to Stage 2, exponential development, institutions of higher education will need to change their methods of planning. Continuing to use the remnants of the McNamara planning process will lead higher education away from continued success, just when the students will need accurate leadership to guide their careers in the digital age.

The purpose of this book is to explain how a continuous, dynamic method of planning can be used when the ten technologies exponentially impact higher education. This method will guide those involved in higher education, including administration, faculty, staff, boards, and most importantly, help students, understand not only what is coming, but also a successful way of working with it. Change is facing higher education. The former industrial model will not work in the digital, exponential age. It is critical that a new method be used, which this book provides.

Leaders in higher education will need to examine the process outlined in the book and make every effort to modify their current planning processes appropriately in order to ensure the viability and success their respective institutions. Data-driven decision making will have to be made in shorter time frames. Long-range planning will use visioning looking out a decade or more, goals will be reduced to a year or two, and short-range objectives will be completed in a matter of weeks or months.

This book provides a planning method that is specifically focused on institutions of higher education and one which will work in a rapidly changing, digital world. It is well worth the time and effort it takes to understand and put it to use.

Chapter One

Toboggan Theory

It was winter in southwestern Michigan. As usual, the month of January was cloudy most of the time and cold consistently. Outside the temperature ranged from just above zero to the teens. Snow two feet deep lay quietly covering the ground with drifts created by the wind reaching three feet high. Groups of high schoolers often congregated on the snow-covered hills at a local golf course in the late afternoon. One or two of them brought ten-foot wooden stripped toboggans with a turned up front end that circled around toward the rear at about 240 degree angle.

WINTER FUN FOR GROUPS

The groups were usually made up of young people who came to have a good time together, as tobogganing is not a single person's sport. It demands a group of six to eight people who most likely know each other or want to get to know those in the group. All are dressed in jeans or snow pants, with heavy, warm coats, waterproof gloves or mittens, stocking caps or another warm type of head covering, and boots. They are ready for an exciting time together on a snowy afternoon. They are aware that tobogganing is a team effort in which they will work together to make things happen.

Toboggans and Sleds

The toboggan itself is much different from a sled with its two runners. Sleds are controlled by pulling on a handle located about a foot behind the sled's front edge of two steel runners. When the handle is pulled to the right or left it causes the sled to turn in one direction or the other. When sliding down a hill, the rider has pretty good control of the direction of the sled and can quite easily keep from striking others who are sledding or missing a protruding obstacle like a tree.

The toboggan on the other hand is designed to slide forward in a straight line. It can be turned right or left by the person in front pulling up on the circular part at the front of the toboggan toward the right or left, an action which creates a minimal veering in a new direction, but nothing very spectacular. In other words, those in the toboggan have to decide where they want to end up at the end of the run with the possibility of making minor adjustments to the direction as it moves down the hill. It might be able to keep the toboggan from hitting an obstacle, but it is not going to make a sharp, right-hand turn.

Tobogganing as a Team Sport

A team of about six to eight people are needed for a rapid ride from the top to the bottom of the hill. After the toboggan is situated at the edge of the hill, the lead person sits cross legged in the front. The second person sits right against the lead person with his or her legs wrapped around the lead person with the boots tucked in between the cross legs of the lead person. Once the first two are settled, the third person gets on behind the second rider with his or her legs wrapped around the second person and the boots tucked in between that person's legs. The others repeat the process as they get on. When all are properly situated, the ride downhill can begin.

To operate a toboggan everyone involved has to work together in preparation for the downhill slide. It takes a few minutes, but once the team is ready, everyone hangs on to each other or to a rope that runs from the front of the toboggan to the rear at the outside edges. The entire setup gets quite friendly so that it was common for riders to seat themselves boy-girl. When the last person was settled into place, another person or two give the loaded toboggan a push, down the hill it would go, picking up speed as it went until it hit the bottom and the ride gradually came to a halt.

When the toboggan came to a standstill, everyone would untangle themselves, stand up, discuss the excitement of the ride down, pull the toboggan up the hill, and reload. Often the toboggan would go down the same track making a groove that with a few rides which would help it to speed up and lengthen the distance at the bottom before it came to a stop. Other times the toboggan would make a new downhill track with snow flying everywhere including directly into the faces of those on board.

Toboggan Business

For groups who were really serious about tobogganing, there were private companies who created concrete chutes a few inches wider than the toboggan with a curb on each side. These chutes were located on the downside of a high hill. During the winter, water was trickled down the chute to freeze until there was about an inch or more of ice on the chute. When all was properly prepared, the toboggan was placed at the top edge of the down slope of the chute.

After everyone got on and was settled, the toboggan was pushed forward. Then the ride of roller-coaster speed of 60 miles per hour or more was soon experienced by all as the toboggan slid down the ice-covered chute. At the bottom the riders untangled themselves and stood up. A motor-powered rope was used by the participants to get themselves pulled back to the top of the hill, where they reloaded and slid down the hill again.

TOBOGGANING AND PLANNING

Tobogganing and planning for higher education in the twenty-first century have a lot in common. The teamwork, speed, repetition, and results combine to make both into experiences that fulfills a definite need, whether sliding to the bottom of a hill or planning for the future. Both will demand working as a team in a specific manner. Both understand the need for high velocity. Both find value in repetition, and both work to create successful results.

The following chapters will discuss how strategic planning in the twenty-first century impacted by technologies can best be completed with ongoing, dynamic, repetitious, high-velocity teamwork. Planning is no longer a closed circuit process, an all-under-one-roof method. That model of linear planning is no longer of much use. Rather, an exponential planning process is needed to work successfully with the technological disruptions of the current century. Success in planning for higher education will require a significant change in understanding, planning, and action.

CONCLUSION

This book will discuss the changing planning environment created by ten technologies developing in the twenty-first century. The very act of planning for the future success of higher education in the United States will require a significant change in the method used to develop vision, goals, and objectives that will allow it to remain successful in the future. The twenty-first century will see technological changes that will impact life, work, learning, and higher education as it is known today. It is critical that those involved community colleges and universities understand the impending changes and serial disruptions that will occur and learn how to deal with them successfully for all concerned.

CHAPTER 1 SUMMARY

- Tobogganing is a fun winter sport.
- Tobogganing takes a group to operate.
- The toboggan differs from the sled in terms of how it is controlled.
- Tobogganing is a team sport that creates downhill speed and enjoyment.
- Proper seating in a toboggan is critical.
- It requires a team approach.

- Tobogganing is a repetitive sport in that the team slides downhill, untangles themselves, walks together back to the top of the hill, re-entwines on the toboggan, and repeats the slide.
- Private businesses developed longer concrete chutes the toboggan used to slide down very rapidly.
- Tobogganing and planning for higher education in the twenty-first century have a lot in common.
- Both tobogganing and twenty-first century planning require teamwork, speed, and repetition to create successful results.
- The very act of planning for the future success of higher education will require a significant change in the method used to develop goals and objectives to remain successful in the future.

Chapter Two

Higher Education at the Precipice

As higher education is heading toward the end of the first quarter of the twenty-first century, changes caused by technological development are imminent. There are ten technologies that are developing in a two-stage process: Stage 1, linear development and Stage 2, exponential development. Briefly, Stage 1 moves ahead in a day-by-day, month-by-month, and year-by-year process. The development of the automobile in the twentieth century is a good example. The gasoline engine was invented in the late nineteenth century. It was soon applied to existing horse-drawn carriages, which allowed individuals to ride in a carriage powered by a mechanical engine rather than being pulled by a horse.

REACTION TO THE EARLY HORSELESS CARRIAGES

When those first gasoline-powered vehicles appeared on the scene, most people were not certain what to make of the noisy, smoky contraptions. Although some individuals at the time may have envisioned many more of those rattletraps invading the neighborhoods, most understood them as brief playthings that would soon go the way of other strange inventions that appeared in the late nineteenth century. However, there were a few individuals who could see real possibilities in the invention of a small engine powering a horseless carriage. One was Henry Ford.

Ford worked a number of times on attaching a four-cycle gasoline engine to a carriage experimentally. His efforts started with a series of failures to which he assigned the letters, a, b, c, and so on. His success came when he put together a version he described with the letter t. The Ford Model T became a producible engine-powered vehicle. When Ford added the assembly line to the manufacturing process, he created huge numbers of a very successful automobile which he built and sold by the thousands for decades. His Model T evolved very gradually and changed only slightly from year to year. Ford actually claimed that the car came in any color as long as it was black. The process he used was linear, one year at a time.

TWENTY-FIRST-CENTURY INVENTORS

Uber

Fast forward to the twenty-first century. Two men, Travis Kalanick and Garrett Camp, had an idea. In 2007, they decided to start a private cab company called UberCab (O'Connell, 2019). After they began it, they were sued for including the word "cab" in the name of their company and lost the suit in court. With some further thinking they came to a conclusion that they might be more successful with a slightly different version of their original idea. They wondered if people would be interested in using cars they owned, which set unused in their garages, as a transportation system to take other people from one place to another.

To find out, they decided on the business idea of Uber and used computer power to help manage it. From 2008 to about 2011, Uber developed in Stage 1, the linear stage. During its Stage 1 development, no one paid much attention to it, not even the taxi industry. However, when Stage 2, exponential development, was reached in about 2012, Uber expanded in an unexpected velocity. Uber became on overnight sensation; people actually were interested in using their cars as a transportation system for other people. Its developmental speed was beyond anything expected or had been experienced in the past; it was Stage 2, exponential.

Disruptions in the Taxi Industry

It seemed to those in the taxi industry that the disruption to their business caused by Uber had come from nowhere. Taxi businesses and drivers were at a loss to understand what had happened. Further, they found they could come up with very little to stop the intense competition that Uber created for them. There was no way to stop Uber through lawsuits, nor were the state and city regulations that governed the taxi business applicable to control the expansion. Uber had found a void in the regulated taxi transportation system as individual car owners giving someone a ride, even for pay, was not a taxi business as legally understood.

The taxi business could only continue on as best it could while watching much of its customer base disappear. From the higher education perspective, imagine for a moment what might have happened if the MOOC approach to education had worked. Suddenly, out of nowhere higher education would be stood on its head just like the taxi industry. However, MOOCs did not work that way, but perhaps it could have in different circumstances. Other competitive ideas for higher education may come to the surface at any time, particularly if the leaders in community colleges and universities are not paying attention.

The Stage 1 World

Looking back historically for just a moment, consider what might have happened to the Ford Motor Company if Henry Ford, who worked his entire life in Stage 1, linear development, had Stage 2 to work with. If Ford had been aware of the Stage 2 possibilities, Ford car development would have moved ahead at breakneck speed and perhaps the Mustang car may have become a reality in the late 1920s.

However, he and his company had no choice but to remain in Stage 1 because a critically important ingredient that propels new ideas ahead at an exponential velocity today did not exist in a usable fashion in the early twentieth century—the computer. The best he might have had to work with was adding machines and early versions of the typewriter.

Both could do the job needed, but at a phenomenally slower and much more expensive pace because of the manpower involved.

Airbnb

Another example of the two-stage development is Airbnb. In 2007, three men, Brian Chesky, Joe Gebbia, and Nathan Blecharczyk, were going to travel to a conference but came up short for the cost of their housing at the conference. It got them to thinking about how to deal with their dilemma and they came up with a solution. Two of them decided to rent out a room in their apartment in order to help pay for the trip. As the story goes, they had an extra room and an airbed. The rental worked out and it sparked an even better idea. These men designed a process whereby people could rent out an extra room or rooms in their homes and provide breakfast in the morning for the overnight renters (Aydin, 2019).

They initially called their idea Air Bed and Breakfast, but soon abbreviated it to Airbnb. They had no reason to believe that the notion would go anywhere, but they took a shot to see what would happen. To their surprise, the idea worked beyond their wildest expectations. In a very few years, Airbnb spread from one state to the next and it was not long before it was national phenomenon. From there, it went international. As it turned out, there were literally thousands of people who had rooms to rent.

It was an idea that seemed a bit far-fetched, as bed and breakfast homes already existed across the country. However, the idea became a reality because individual homeowners were interested in making some money on the side by putting a room and breakfast on the market. Given the interest it uncovered throughout the United States and internationally, Airbnb expanded exponentially in Stage 2 because it had digital support. Computer power added to a speculative idea created a move to Stage 2 in a very short period of time, an exponential phenomenon.

Amazon

As a third example, consider Jeff Bezos and Amazon. In the late 1990s, the company joined the dot-com bubble when it began selling books online. It found a market void and did very well in that business. So well, in fact, that some major booksellers went out of business because of the competition Amazon created. Who wanted to use the tried and true Sears, Roebuck, Montgomery Ward, J.C. Penney method of seeing a picture in a catalog of a purchasable product and be able to buy it by viewing the product on the Internet and have it delivered to their home? It turned out, millions of people did.

Jeff Bezos, like Henry Ford with his Model T, had a very good book business going, but Bezos saw an opportunity to exponentially increase his. He already had the computer support for his existing business, so he expanded the company to selling almost anything online. In just a few years Amazon moved to Stage 2. Today it competes with major retailers across the country and the world. At the foundation of that business is digital capabilities. Without it, Bezos may have developed a good business, but not the one that made him a billionaire with millions of customers.

Because of digital support, the three ideas became phenomenally successful business realities in very short periods of time. Today, Uber is the largest people transportation system in the world; Airbnb is the largest provider of rooms in the world, and Amazon may not be the largest, but it probably is a close second to whatever is in the retail world. What did the founders of these three businesses need in addition to a good idea? Powerful computers and software. Without digital support, Uber, Airbnb, and Amazon may have remained good ideas that most likely would have never seen the light of day.

On the other side of that coin, bookstores, department store chains, and even big box stores are struggling, faltering, and some are closing. When a consumer goes to many retail stores today, it is likely that the checkout is done almost totally by computer. Fast food businesses are not far behind. Closing in on them will be any job a computer or a robot can do, like pharmacy work counting medications, nursing home work, and accountants, just to name a few. Interestingly, South Korea is already experimenting with classroom robot teachers, which they demonstrated in the 2018 Winter Olympics.

ROBOTS AND EDUCATION

What is the future of robot instruction? Today, it is at best only a fascination, a dream, an idea. Most would think it is merely science fiction that would be good for the movie industry. However, what about young people interested in education who might make an effort to see what else could be done? Or what about an existing company which was willing to take a risk and develop the robot teacher that really worked well with students and the learning process? What then? Are existing educational leaders on the lookout for such a thing to happen?

It is critically important to understand that twenty-first-century technologies are going to develop along that Two-Stage trajectory. On the other hand, it is not as obvious to see what kinds of jobs will be added to replace those lost. Some of the foreseeable new jobs are cybersecurity, robot repair, and robot programming. However, many others will arrive in reaction to or support of the technological disruptions. The business community is researching the technologies to support increased production, speed, quality, and profits. Business leaders know that they must keep up with the latest developments in technology because if they do not, global competition will push them to the side. New jobs will be created that are not even imagined today.

Amazon, Airbnb, and Uber are harbingers of what is to come when ten technologies, supported by the digital age, evolve to the exponential Stage 2. Autonomous cars, 3D printing, the Internet of Things, personal robots, medical genome, agricultural genome, Bitcoin/Blockchain, quantum computing, artificial intelligence, and nanotechnology are all currently developing in Stage 1. Observers know they exist; however, they may not be aware of the fact that all of them will move to Stage 2 in the near future.

STAGE TWO AND HIGHER EDUCATION

What will the effect of Stage 2 be on higher education? In general terms, a great deal of rapid, serial disruptions. Community college and university administrators, faculty, and staff must be prepared to deal successfully with those technologies that will impact them. They will have to be re-educated to be able to deal successfully with the digital, exponential world that faces them. The linear *Model T* experience will be replaced with the *Amazon-Airbnb-Uber* exponential phenomenon.

TEN TECHNOLOGIES AND STAGE 2

What faces higher education by the middle of the twenty-first century? For certain, the ten technologies that are developing in Stage 1, all of which will move to Stage 2 by 2050, most, long before that. Table 2.1 displays the estimates of when each of the ten technologies will move to Stage 2 with the accompanying exponential development.

Table 2.1. Estimates of When the Technologies Will Move to Stage 2

Technology	Stage 2 Prediction
Agricultural Genome Development	2025–2030
The Internet of Things	2025–2030
Personal Robots	2025–2030
Quantum Computing	2025–2030
3D Printing	2030–2035
Artificial Intelligence	2030–2035
Autonomous Cars	2030–2035
Bitcoin/Blockchain	2030–2035
Human Genome Technology	2030–2035
Nanotechnology	2040–2045

With that set of estimates in mind, the following takes a brief look at the technologies and when they are most likely to move to Stage 2. If these estimates are accurate, a good number of serial disruptions to the business community, health organizations, and higher education are developing behind the scenes, preparing to happen. This is no time to sit back with a wait-and-see attitude; the present is the time to begin the preparation for the serial disruptions the ten technologies will create when they hit Stage 2.

Agricultural Genome Development

Agricultural genome development has the potential to design crops that are resistant to disease, faster growing, and have increased food value. The amount of product per acre can be significantly increased as well. The ability to increase the amount and the health value of foods will become critical to farming because of the projected tremendous increase in population on the Earth by the year 2050. Current food production will need to double to keep up with the growth. Very significant changes are on the near horizon in the food production arena.

The Internet of Things

The Internet of Things (IoT), a method of collecting data using RFID sensors the size of a grain of rice, which can be into or on just about anything manufactured, is well on its way along Stage 1. It is estimated that the number of specific pieces of data collected will be in the trillions by the mid-2020s (Miller, 2015). Each sensor will relay data to the cloud where it will be stored and can be accessed by interested parties. This means that any product that is manufactured with embedded RFID sensors will store information that would be of interest to the manufacturer in terms of the lifespan of the product and its internal parts. Improvements could be made in future products based on the data already collected. No need to wait and do a survey.

Retailers would also be interested in the data. It would allow them to understand which products are of greatest interest to the consumer, how the product compares to competitive products, and how to make decisions as to which products to obtain and place in the retail establishment. Additionally, consumers will be interested in the data as they prepare to make a purchase. That data may be made available directly to the consumer, or it may be accessed through written reports or videos on the products. What is most important is that the data will be available in real time.

In addition, it is fully within the realm of possibilities that new, unimagined businesses will spring up that use and distribute information gleaned from the data-filled clouds. Entrepreneurs are already looking seriously into the potential for starting businesses and making money from the trillions of data collected on almost any manufactured product.

Personal Robots

Personal Robots have the potential to completely change living and lifestyles. Countries such as Japan and South Korea are far down the Stage 1 path already. Other countries like Germany, France, the UK, and the United States are not far behind. When the production of personal robots move to Stage 2, they will suddenly be available globally. If Americans are not too interested in developing them, other countries will produce them in rapid order.

Japan started developing personal robots in about 2005. They had a very definite reason to do so. Because of their diet, which is very healthy, Japanese individuals tend to live longer. In addition, it is very difficult to immigrate to Japan. It is a small country filled with mountains with very limited space to live and thrive, which resulted in controls affecting how many humans could be allowed to immigrate into the country. The Japanese faced a growing population of aging citizens without the appropriate number of young people to provide the care the seniors are going to need.

As a solution, they decided to create personal robots which could provide the care needed for its aging population. They are a long way down the road on that development. The Honda car company created ASIMO, which can do a number of activities as well as communicate verbally. Other companies developed personal robots that look and act like real people.

South Korea too has also gone down the personal robot pathway. During the 2018 Winter Olympics they used 80 robots. Ten humanoid robots, each about three feet high, skied down a slope. Others did various kinds of work including carrying the torch, polishing floors, and painting murals, and teaching students in the classroom.

China has gotten into the personal robot arena with a variety of robots for different functions, including a comical one: a robot pulling a rickshaw. The United States, especially in the military, is creating personal robot prototypes as well, including robots with four legs looking somewhat like a dog, which can be used to carry heavy equipment over various terrains. Countries in Europe are doing similar personal robot development, such as providing home security, house-cleaning, street cleaning, a variety of toys, and other functions. Personal robots will appear as quickly as they can be imagined, designed, built, and sold.

Personal robots are developing in Stage 1, but do not assume they are of no concern. Consumers might be interested in having a personal robot that looked human, which could, for example, clean the house, work in the yard, prepare meals, order food supplies, and wash the dishes. Soon everyone could have their own personal robots; it is only a matter of time. The third decade of the twenty-first century will see this technology move ahead very rapidly and many robots will be ready for purchase before 2030. Big box retail stores will be selling them.

By the mid-2030s personal robots could be a mainstay on higher education campuses. They can provide a number of daily, repetitive chores, such as providing receptionist duties, cleaning the facilities, mowing the lawns, doing maintenance projects, and providing security. If the job is repetitive and routine, robots could take over many those kinds of jobs on campuses. It will be interesting to see how soon robot assistants will join teachers in the classroom.

Quantum Computing

In September 2019, Google announced that it had developed a quantum computer (Porter, 2019). This was a gargantuan step on Google's part. Although predictions for an initial operational quantum computer was expected sometime in the late 2020s, the fact that Google created one in 2019 is extremely impressive. This kind of computing uses atoms rather than silicon chips. Computing in that way puts the scientists involved into a totally different environment. The speed and accuracy of quantum computing compared to silicon chip computing is so great that it is difficult to come up with a comparison metaphor.

The Quantum Environment

The quantum environment is difficult to understand because it is so different from the world humans live in on a daily basis. Newton's Laws very accurately describe the visible, existing world and what is known of the universe. To step into the quantum environment is beyond anything experienced in the perceivable world. Even Albert Einstein spent much of his life in opposition to thinking that the quantum environment was totally different from the observable world. However, other twentieth-century scientists proved the quantum world to be totally different (Isaacson, 2007). When dealing with things at the atom level, Newton's Laws do not explain anything. Quantum laws, so to speak, guide another environment altogether.

Quantum physicists have determined that atoms exist in two places at the same time. They can be close to each other or extremely far apart. No matter the distance, they stay connected to each other. This sounds strange because humans do not live in that kind of environment. Living on earth as humans do, Newton's Laws work quite well. However, at the atomic level, Newton's Laws are literally thrown out the window. Scientists working in the quantum world can take advantage of the fact that two atoms are connected no matter the distance (Johnson, 2003).

In the classical computer that is used daily, the processor works with bits. There are ones and zeroes. Transistors handle that difference by turning off or on. In the quantum computer, the bits are replaced with quantum bit or qubits. A qubit is made up of a pair of atoms. Each pair has not one set of ones and zeroes but a myriad of sets. Using atoms makes a phenomenal difference in how fast the computer can operate. When qubits are connected with each other, the computing power expands in an exponential manner and it makes Moore's Law look like it is moving in reverse (Johnson, 2003).

Classical vs. Quantum Computing

In an attempt to understand the difference between classical computing and quantum computing, consider this scenario. If all the information collected since the first recorded history of mankind were put into today's classical computer storage, it would take a multi-storied storage facility located on the distance of about six blocks. In the quantum computer, that same amount of information would take up less than half the size of a printed period at that end of a sentence. While that is hard to comprehend, it is true in the quantum world.

Because quantum computing is so important, the Chinese are investing an estimated $10 billion in a $4 million square foot facility that will deal only with quantum metrology and quantum computing. The facility is planned to be completed in 2020. Its completion could put China in a very powerful position in terms of quantum computing. Americans can be thankful that Google and IBM are already far down the path to useable quantum computing because it is a game-changer in the world of computing.

Quantum computing is being developed rapidly through Stage 1 and when it jumps to Stage 2, which could happen by the mid-2020s, the computing world will be turned upside down. The business world, health community, and the military are anticipating the Stage 2 development and will be ready to learn how to use it. It no doubt will impact higher education significantly as well. It is best for all concerned to be as prepared as possible for the movement of quantum computing to its second stage.

3D Printing

3D printing, also known as additive manufacturing, already has a significant history. A grand variety of small objects have been created from plastic and metals. Entire car bodies and internal components of automobile engines have been produced. Most interesting is the fact house construction can be completed using additive manufacturing. Today a concrete additive-manufactured house can be produced in a matter of days for considerably less cost than standard home construction. In addition, the exterior walls are much stronger than wood frame or brick, so much so that they can withstand hurricane winds. The future for this type of house construction has real possibilities.

Christopher Barnett, author of *3D Printing*, in its third edition since 2013, estimates that 3D printing will have made a significant impact on manufacturing by the late 2020s to the early 2030s. He estimates that by 2033, some 20 percent of products manufactured will be partially or totally created by 3D printing, or additive manufacturing (Barnett, 2016). The Chinese are also working on 3D printing at a ferocious rate. They have already developed a series of additive manufactured houses, which they can produce in rapid order. In Mexico, entire housing subdivisions are being constructed with additive manufacturing because of the low cost and durability.

There are some construction companies in the United States that have begun work with additive manufactured housing, but so far what has been produced is only in small numbers. When the strength, low cost, and speed of construction is taken into consideration, additive manufacturing is a product waiting to happen. When it develops to Stage 2, the housing business may see a very significant, rapid disruption of current housing construction methods.

Artificial General Intelligence

In 1997, artificial intelligence was used in the computer Deep Blue when it beat the multi-year chess champion Garry Kasparov in chess for the first time (Kasparov, 2017). In 2011, Watson, another highly advanced computer, beat the two best players in *Jeopardy* (Baker, 2011). Both Deep Blue and Watson are what is called Narrow AI—Narrow Artificial Intelligences—because they each could do one thing: create the strategy to win at chess or win at *Jeopardy*.

Watson Computer

However, the Watson computer has since been reprogrammed to work in the medical world, and other fields. Watson was inputted with a great deal of medical data on the subject of cancer, which has been used it to support the work of oncologists. It was soon found that the Watson computer often came to better conclusions faster than most doctors could. Medical artificial intelligence is still a narrow AI because is cannot take action with a patient, but is used as rapid, accurate input to the doctor. Add quantum computing to the Watson and its power and velocity would increase dramatically.

In the near future, the capabilities of the Watson computer will undoubtedly change and mature. For example, a Watson computer hooked up to a medical robot in the future might perform many procedures now completed by a human being. This development could make considerable changes in medicine as currently understood and practiced. Imagine going to the doctor's office and being told by the robot receptionist that the robot physician's assistant will see you prior to speaking with the doctor. Such a change is possible in the near future.

Further, there is another thing that will develop much sooner. Moore's Law suggests that computer power and storage doubles every 18–24 months. That kind of doubling could lead to the possibility of a computer with an intellect equal to a human being in all aspects. That possibility was initially predicted to happen by futurist Ray Kurzweil by 2045 (Kurzweil, 2005). He and other futurists agree that the time is coming in the next few decades when a computer will be able to think like a human being. With quantum computing now in play, Kurzweil modified his prediction to 2030.

Beyond Narrow AI

Beyond narrow AI as now experienced, Artificial General Intelligence (AGI), a computer with mental abilities equal to a human being, could exist by 2030, with possible IQ of 300. If Moore's Law continues for just a few years after the AGI becomes a reality, the next step will be the development of an Artificial Super Intelligence (ASI) with an IQ of perhaps 1 million or more. However, by 2030 or earlier, quantum computing could provide the possibility of an Artificial General Intelligence.

With quantum computing, Artificial Super Intelligence with an IQ in the millions could come on the scene by 2035. That is absolutely phenomenal. The changes such a mentality could bring is beyond words to describe. If Kurzweil is correct in his estimate, it is no wonder that the possibility keeps physicists, scientists, IT personnel, military leaders, and others up at night worrying about what comes next.

Artificial Super Intelligence

Some futurists are concerned that an Artificial Super Intelligence may bring a rapid end to the human race. Other futurists think humans would adapt to the increased mental power of the AGI and ASI by becoming cyborgs, having pieces and parts of the computer placed on or in our brains and bodies (Barfield, 2015). In that way humans could keep up with the computer and/or computerized robots on a level playing field. It is a possibility, but will that work to benefit human beings? There is no way to know in advance. The supposition would be that one could pull the plug on the computer if it did not work; however, even that is not known for certain.

Should humans today stop the AGI computer from ever being built? The positive answer to that question seems like a good idea. However, that positive decision is probably not possible. If the United States decided against AGI and ASI, what is there to stop other countries from moving ahead full speed to develop such a mentality? The argument may be that it is in the United States' best interest to develop the AGI and its descendant, the ASI. At least then the AGI/ASI would be best understood and hopefully be beneficial to mankind.

Autonomous Cars

Autonomous cars have the potential to ultimately end self-driven cars as they move to Stage 2. Whether that extreme will take place is difficult to determine. How soon that could happen is another difficult question to answer. After the horseless carriage became all the rage, horses did not disappear, nor did horse racing. Today all major car manufacturers and other businesses like Google and Apple are creating useable autonomous car models. Tesla has been in the forefront for a number of years now, but other car companies like Ford, Chevrolet, Chrysler, BMW, Rolls-Royce, Mazda, Hyundai, and others are catching up in rapid manner.

Obstacles Facing Autonomous Cars

At present there are three obstacles facing the autonomous car development: insurance issues, federal/state regulations, and consumer interest. In terms of insurance issues, if the car is totally autonomous, who is responsible if there is an accident with another vehicle, or worse, a person? Is the responsible party the manufacturer, the retailer, the people sitting the car, or who? The answer to that question has the potential to change insurance policies considerably. It will most likely take some time and effort on the part of the insurance businesses. One hopes they are already working on their new policies and not taking a wait-and-see posture.

Federal and state regulations that currently govern person-driven vehicles will also need to change. For instance, what about an autonomous car that goes over the speed limit, runs a red light, or stalls on the highway stopping traffic? What changes will be needed in regulations to these simple questions and, undoubtedly, much more complicated ones that need written policies? Back when the horseless carriages were first on the road, in some locations a person had to be walking in front of the car warning others of the potential danger that a vehicle was coming that would surprise them and frighten their horses. Laws soon followed back then. What about now?

Perhaps the biggest obstacle may be the consumers. Do they want to accept autonomous cars? Will they want to purchase one or only rent them when needed? After all, many persons love driving their own vehicles. Just because autonomous vehicles are available does not mean there will be an immediate collective consensus by the consumer. It may take an entire generation for the acceptance to spread widely throughout the United States and the rest of the world.

Urban dwellers in large metropolitan areas may be the first to accept autonomous, rented vehicles since they are already used to busses, taxis, Uber, and subways. Those living in rural areas may move much slower to autonomous transportation. This issue will most likely take time to be worked out, but Americans did learn how to do without their horses and accept the early automobile alternative in not much more than a decade or two. In today's rapidly changing world, acceptance might come sooner rather than later. Time will tell.

Bitcoin/Blockchain

Another technology to consider, which is getting mixed press at the moment, is Bitcoin/Blockchain. This is an alternative financial system that was brought onto the scene in 2008. It uses digital money called Bitcoins. Basically one purchases a Bitcoin with dollars, Euros, Yens, or other monetary forms. The purchase ends up as a set of numbers in a digital ledger. The block ledgers are protected with cryptography so the ledgers cannot be altered once made (Tapscott, 2016). At least that was the thinking of those who created the system.

Hackers Disruption

However, a few years ago a hacker found a weakness in the digital procedure and made away with millions of Bitcoins. Supposedly that situation was solved, but it does not mean that a future hacker won't find another way to upset the system for monetary advantage. In addition, it was learned that the Bitcoin/Blockchain process was being used by those working with illegal methods. Since there is no bank or federal agency that oversees the Bitcoin/Blockchain process, as it is self-regulated, there most likely will be reluctance in accepting it by the consumer.

Understand that Bitcoin/Blockchain is something that exists in the cloud and can only be accessed by the owners. The process remains in Stage 1 and still has much improvement to be made to it, but it exists and is being used by individuals globally and experimented with by financial institutions. If the issues it faces become ameliorated, it most likely will become a new form of finance.

Human Genome Development

Human genome development has already entered the classrooms and labs in biology courses with the study of Clustered Regularity Interspaced, Short Palindromic Repeats, CRISPR, which is a method for modifying genomes. Soon after the CRISPR process was created, it was significantly speeded up with further research which led to the enzyme Cas9. Today the process is known as CRISPR/Cas9. It allows genes to be moved, deleted and/or added, easily and quickly (Doudna, 2017).

Since many diseases have genome connections, the ability to change the gene structure has the potential to cure many afflictions now affecting human beings. Already there is work being done in the medical fields of cancer, heart disease, arthritis, birth defects, diabetes, and sickle cell anemia, with more to come (Doudna, 2017). In addition, CRISPER/Cas9 provides a method that could be used to create designer babies. Parents could make decisions as to which genes to delete that may have medical issues in the families previous to the present, and which genes to add that may have to do with facial features, muscular abilities, or mental capabilities. The possibilities are many.

Nanotechnology

Nanotechnology is developing offstage on a number of fronts. This technology allows for the development of products made at the level of atoms. At present, the working conditions when dealing with atoms require near absolute zero (minus 400 degrees Fahrenheit), which restricts the necessary working environment. In addition, there is a danger of the atoms moving right through the flesh of a human being. No one is sure what kind of issues that might create (Drexler, 1986).

On the other side of the coin, nanotechnology would allow any country in the world who could obtain the equipment, develop the proper environment, and hire the expertise to work with atoms to produce most anything it wanted to with no natural resources, other than the ubiquitous atom. It would take a considerable amount of scientific education combined with an unusual and expensive environment; nonetheless, the opportunity would exist. Most likely any country which wanted to could get involved with the process.

ON THE PRECIPICE

So where does this put higher education from community college to the university in the United States with education and training? It puts them all on the precipice. Higher education finds itself at the top of the toboggan chute, ready to be nudged over the edge to a very rapid drop with a lot of excitement all the way to the bottom. When the ride slows to a stop at the bottom of the hill, the entire system of higher education will have to unpack, get to its feet, grab the rope and get pulled back to the top for another ride.

However, the next ride to the bottom may be different. This time the impact of autonomous cars reaching Stage 2 will go along for the ride. As the staff and faculty got on the toboggan at the top of the hill, they were discussing how these cars will affect the community college. As they zipped down the hill conversations were replaced with yells. After they unpacked again at the bottom and walked back up holding onto the rope, they began to talk about planning for the institution. After a couple more rides they decided to meet at a local restaurant and there they talked more about the opportunities that autonomous cars would provide.

As they talked, it dawned on them that they may have come upon a method for planning for the institution and decided to talk more about it at work the next week. What they envisioned were groups who would investigate the technologies to see where the data led them. They wanted data-driven decision making and leadership. They thought committees might work best, just like when they were packed onto the toboggan. They understood that collecting information and relaying it to those in charge had to be done in rapid order. With ten technologies, the rides down the chute would be often and would have to be productive.

Toboggan theory: pack the team together, hold on tight for the ride, unpack at the bottom, and discuss your way to the top. Repeat as often as needed. Write up the conclusions based on data. From there, take action as needed. No time to spare. Exponential development in Stage 2 requires exponential thinking on the part of all concerned. This book will describe just how that works.

CONCLUSION

It is critical that higher education institutions get fully involved in learning how to deal with the ten technologies they are facing. It will take a process to successfully plan on how to effectively use the technologies for the benefit of community college and university administration, faculty, staff, and students. It will not be an easy set of tasks. It will be working with serial disruptions of considerable magnitude, and will take careful, accurate planning.

CHAPTER 2 SUMMARY

- At the end of the first quarter of the twenty-first century, changes caused by technological development are imminent.
- There are ten technologies that are developing in a two-stage process: Stage 1, linear development and Stage 2, exponential development.
- The development of the automobile in the twentieth century is a good example of Stage 1 development.
- Henry Ford could see real possibilities with the invention of a small engine powering a horseless carriage.
- The Ford Model T became a producible engine-powered vehicle.
- His Model T evolved very gradually and changed only slightly from year to year.
- The process he used was linear, one year at a time.
- Two men, Travis Kalanick and Garrett Camp had an idea.
- In 2007, they started a private cab company called UberCab.
- When UberCab did not work out, they wondered if people would be interested in using cars they owned as a transportation system to take people from one place to another.
- When Uber reached Stage 2 in about 2012, it expanded in an exponential manner.
- Taxi businesses and drivers were at a loss to understand what had happened.

- There was no way to stop Uber through lawsuits, nor were the state and city regulations that governed the taxi business applicable to control the expansion.
- Uber had found a void in the regulated taxi transportation system.
- From the higher education perspective, imagine for a moment what might have happened if the MOOC approach to education had worked.
- Other competitive ideas for higher education may come to the surface at any time.
- If Henry Ford had been able to use Stage 2 possibilities, the Mustang car might have been a reality in the late-1920s.
- The lack of computer power kept Henry Ford from moving into Stage 2.
- Another example of the two-stage development is Airbnb.
- Three men, Brian Chesky, Joe Gebbia, and Nathan Blecharczyk, designed a process whereby people could rent out extra rooms in their homes and provide breakfast in the morning for the overnight renters.
- In a very short time Airbnb spread from one state to the next and it was not long before it was national phenomenon.
- Airbnb could expand exponentially in Stage 2 because it had digital support.
- Jeff Bezos already had the computer support for his book business, so he expanded the company to selling almost anything online.
- Today, Uber is the largest people transportation system in the world; Airbnb is the largest provider rooms in the world, and Amazon may not be the largest, but it probably is a close second to whatever is in the retail world.
- Without digital support, Uber, Airbnb, and Amazon may have remained good ideas that most likely never saw the light of day.
- On the other side of that coin, bookstores, department store chains, and even big box stores are struggling, faltering, some are closing up shop.
- South Korea is already experimenting with classroom robot teachers.
- What is the future of robot instruction?

- Are existing educational leaders on the lookout for such a thing to happen?
- It is not as obvious to see what kinds of jobs will be added to replace those lost.
- Some of the foreseeable jobs are cybersecurity, robot repair, and robot programming.
- Others will arrive in reaction to or support of the technological disruptions.
- The three examples presented above are the harbingers of what is to come when ten technologies, supported by the digital age, evolve to the exponential Stage 2.
- What will the effect of Stage 2 be on higher education?
- In general terms, a great deal of rapid, serial disruptions.
- Higher Education leaders, faculty, and staff will have to be re-educated.
- The Model T experience will be replaced with the Uber-Airbnb-Amazon phenomenon.
- There are ten technologies developing in Stage 1, all of which will move to Stage 2 by 2050, most, long before that time.
- Agricultural genome development has the potential to design crops that are resistant to disease, faster growing, and increasing food value.
- The Internet of Things (IoT), a method of collecting data using RFID sensors the size of a grain of rice, which can be into or on just about anything manufactured, is well on its way down Stage 1.
- It is fully within the realm of possibilities that new, unimagined businesses will spring up that use and distribute information gleaned from the data-filled clouds.
- Entrepreneurs are already looking seriously into the potential for starting businesses and making money from the trillions of data collected on almost any manufactured product.
- Personal robots have the potential to completely change living and lifestyles.
- Japan started developing personal robots in about 2005.

- The Japanese faced a growing population of aging citizens without the appropriate number of young people to provide the care the seniors are going to need.
- They decided to create personal robots that could provide the care needed for its aging population.
- South Korea too has also gone down the personal robot pathway.
- During the 2018 Winter Olympics they used 80 robots, including a robot teacher.
- China, too, has gotten into the personal robot arena with a variety of robots for different functions, including a robot pulling a rickshaw.
- Countries in Europe are doing similar personal robot development, such as providing home security, house-cleaning, street cleaning, a variety of toys, and other functions.
- The personal robot is developing in Stage 1, but do not assume personal robots are of no concern.
- The third decade of the twenty-first century will see this technology move ahead very rapidly and many robots will be ready for purchase before 2030.
- By the mid-2030s personal robots could be a mainstay on higher education campuses providing a number of daily, repetitive chores, such as providing receptionist duties, cleaning the facilities, mowing the lawns, doing maintenance projects, and providing security.
- In September 2019, Google announced that it had developed a quantum computer.
- The speed and accuracy of quantum computing compared to silicon chip computing is so great that it is difficult to come up with a comparison metaphor.
- To step into the quantum environment is beyond anything experienced in the observable world.
- When dealing with things at the atom level, Newton's Laws do not explain anything.
- Quantum physicists have determined that atoms exist in two places at the same time.
- They can be close to each other or extremely far apart.

- Scientists working in the quantum world can take advantage of the fact that two atoms are connected no matter the distance between them.
- In the quantum computer, the bits are replaced with qubits.
- A qubit is made up of a pair of atoms.
- Each set of atom has not one set of ones and zeros but a myriad of sets.
- If all the information collected since the beginning of today's classical computer storage, it would take a multi-storied facility located on the distance of about six blocks.
- In the quantum computer, that same information would take up less than half the size of a printed period at that end of a sentence.
- Because quantum computing is so important, the Chinese are investing an estimated $10 billion in a $4 million square foot facility that will deal only with quantum metrology and quantum computing.
- The facility is scheduled to be completed in 2020.
- The business world, health community, and the military are anticipating the Stage 2 development and will be ready to learn how to use it.
- 3D printing, also known as additive manufacturing, already has a significant history.
- Most interesting is the fact the house construction can be completed using additive manufacturing.
- In Mexico, entire housing subdivisions are being constructed with additive manufacturing because of the low cost and durability.
- When the strength, low cost, and speed of construction is taken into consideration, additive manufacturing is a product waiting to happen.
- Both Deep Blue and Watson are what is called "narrow AI."
- Narrow Artificial Intelligences because they each could do one thing, create the strategy to win at chess or win at *Jeopardy*.
- Medical Artificial Intelligence is still a narrow AI because is cannot take action with a patient, but is used as rapid, accurate input to the doctor.
- Add quantum computing to the Watson and its power and velocity would increase dramatically.

- A Watson computer hooked up to a medical robot in the future might perform many procedures now completed by a human being.
- Moore's Law suggests that with computer power and storage doubles every 18–24 months.
- That kind of doubling will lead to the possibility of a computer with an intellect equal to a human being in all aspects.
- That was initially predicted to happen by futurist Ray Kurzweil by 2045.
- With quantum computing now in existence, Kurzweil modified his prediction to 2030.
- By 2035 or earlier, quantum computing could provide the possibility of an Artificial Super Intelligence.
- Some futurists are concerned that an Artificial Super Intelligence may bring a rapid end to the human race.
- Other futurists think we would adapt to the increased mental power of the AGI and ASI by becoming cyborgs, having pieces and parts of the computer placed on or in our brains and bodies.
- Should humans today stop the AGI computer from ever being built?
- If the United States decided against AGI and ASI, what is there to stop other countries from moving ahead full speed to develop such a mentality?
- It may be in the country's best interest to develop the AGI and its descendant, the ASI.
- Autonomous cars have the potential to ultimately end self-driven cars as it moves to Stage 2.
- Today all major car manufacturers and other businesses like Google and Apple are creating useable autonomous car models.
- At present there are three obstacles facing the autonomous car development: insurance issues, federal/state regulations, and consumer interest.
- Federal and state regulations that currently govern person-driven vehicles will also need to change.
- For instance, what about an autonomous car that speeds, runs a red light, or stalls on the highway stopping traffic?
- Perhaps the biggest obstacle may be the consumers.
- Do they want to accept autonomous cars?

- Will they want to purchase one or only rent them when needed?
- Urban dwellers in large metropolitan areas may be the first to accept autonomous, rented vehicles since they are already used to busses, taxis, Uber, subways, and the like.
- Those living in rural areas may move much slower to autonomous transportation.
- Another technology to consider, which is getting mixed press at the moment, is Bitcoin/Blockchain.
- This is an alternative financial system that was brought onto the scene in 2008.
- Since there is no bank or federal agency that oversees the Bitcoin/Blockchain process, as it is self-regulated, there most likely will be reluctance in accepting it by the consumer.
- Human genome development has already entered the classrooms and labs in biology courses with the study of Clustered Regularity Interspaced, Short Palindromic Repeats, CRISPR, which is a method for modifying genomes.
- Already there is work being done in the medical fields of cancer, heart disease, arthritis, birth defects, diabetes, and sickle cell anemia, with more to come.
- It is clear that human genome development will provide opportunities for higher education.
- Nanotechnology is developing offstage on a number of fronts. This technology allows for the development of products made at the level of atoms.
- Nanotechnology would allow any country in the world who could obtain the equipment and expertise to work with atoms to produce most anything it wanted to with no natural resources, other than the ubiquitous atom.
- Higher education finds itself at the top of the toboggan chute, ready to be nudged over the edge to a very rapid drop with a lot of excitement all the way to the bottom.
- What they envisioned were groups who would investigate the technologies to see where the data led them.
- They wanted data-driven decision making and leadership.

- Toboggan theory: pack the team together, hold on tight for the ride, unpack at the bottom, and discuss your way to the top.
- It is critical that higher education get fully involved in learning how to deal with the ten technologies they are facing.
- It will be working with serial disruptions of considerable magnitude. It will take careful, accurate planning.

Chapter Three

Technological Impact on Higher Education

Each of the ten technologies discussed earlier in this book will create disruptions in higher education as they move to Stage 2, exponential development. The technologies will reach Stage 2 at different times, some relatively close together, and others farther apart. Exactly when each will transfer itself to Stage 2 is difficult to predict; however, forecasts of an approximate range when each will attain Stage 2 were presented in chapter 2. Reviewing each of the technologies one at a time gives a better idea of what kind of disruption each will create for business/industry, the health community, and higher education when they move to Stage 2.

Dr. Jennifer Doudna (2017) in her book, *A Crack in Creation: Gene Editing and the Unthinkable Power to Control Evolution*, describes the scientific journey she and fellow scientist Dr. Emmanuelle Charpentier traveled to determine how genes could be moved, deleted, or added using a process called Clustered Regularity Interspaced, Short, Palindromic Repeats, (CRISPR), combined with an enzyme Cas9. The potential for developing cures is tremendous. It is what Doudna claims kept her on the track to understand how the genome could be altered for the benefit of the human race (Doudna, 2017).

Knowing that genes control all aspects of the human body is one thing; the ability to move, delete, or add genes to make changes is something altogether different. When Doudna finished her work on genes, she got concerned that maybe she had done the wrong thing as the information from her research could be used for both positive and negative purposes. Now she makes presentations worldwide trying to convince scientists to be careful how they use the CRISPR/Cas9 process (Doudna, 2017).

IMPACT ON HIGHER EDUCATION

Community colleges and universities will be impacted by the need for assistants to be trained at the associate degree level and the need for new medical programs at the university level. In addition, considerable research will be required as the human genome process develops. How well manipulating genomes works on the human being, what types of unforeseen issues arise, and how problems with the technology can be solved for the benefit of mankind are just the beginning of the impact of the technology on higher education.

Agricultural Genome Development

In animal husbandry, finding ways to alter the gene structure is not a new idea as it has been done for centuries by mating the strongest and best farm animals for better results; however, it always took time ranging from years to decades. A great deal of guesswork was involved leading to some beneficial results and many others that were less acceptable. Crossbreeding in the plant world has existed for centuries as well with varied results that in the long run became very significant. Again, experimentation was the method, which did not reveal its results until sometime later.

However, with CRISPR/Cas9, ideas, experiments, and results happen much faster and with less guess work. Plants can be developed that are stronger, disease resistant, and more productive. Grains can be improved to produce more bushels per acre. Given the forecast that by 2050 there will most likely be a huge increase in the population on the earth, the need for more food with greater value is not only a good idea, but will be an absolute necessity. The potential with CRISPR/Cas9 for the increase to happen now exists.

Vertical Farming

Farms operated in a digital manner may also lead to vertical farming. This type of farming is developing in the United States and some countries in Europe. It is an alternative that would take a great deal data to be successful. The digital era could easily give full support to the method.

> Vertical farming is the practice of producing food [indoors], on vertically inclined surfaces. Instead of farming vegetables and other foods on a single layer, such as in a field or greenhouse, this method produces food in vertically stacked layers commonly integrated into other structures like a skyscraper, shipping container or repurposed warehouse. (LeBlanc, 2019)

Vertical farming provides control of the weather as the entire process takes place indoors.

Vertical farming does not use soil as the growing medium as on a normal farm. Instead, it uses aeroponic, aquaponic, or hydroponic mediums for the growing medium (LeBlanc, 2019). Further, light can be brought in from the outside through windows or the enclosed facility can use artificial lighting. Operating in an enclosed, controlled environment calls for considerable computer control of the total environment, which can then produce more food in much less space with great certainty.

In addition, vertical farming could take place near to metropolitan areas, which would reduce the costs transportation of food from farm to market. It truly has the potential to ensure the growth of cities while at the same time reducing the issues with suburban growth. This type of farming may increase significantly in the near future for the benefit of all concerned.

Impact on the University

The impact on universities is considerable as the need for agricultural scientists will increase significantly. New and revised agricultural programs will be needed to meet the demand created by the increased population. The possibilities are tremendous in numbers and types of jobs that will need to be trained for as well as those who teach in the revised and new disciplines. CRISPR/Cas9 is a method to be observed carefully and continuously as it has the potential to change certain segments of the medical community considerably.

Impact on Community Colleges

The impact on community colleges may very well create a resumption of agricultural programs that were deleted. If grain output acre becomes increased significantly, a clear business approach will be needed to operate a successful farm. If vertical farming increases, a digital business method will be necessary. Agricultural programs will become a cross between business programs and digital processes that for classical farming will affect seed selection, fertilizer, cultivation, and water needed per acre. In vertical farming it will affect the growing medium, amount of light, temperature control, humidity control, and more. Successful farming in the future will take more brains than brawn.

The Internet of Things

The Internet of Things (IoT) already exists and is developing robustly in Stage 1. It is mostly behind the curtain and not on full display. The IoT works using radio frequency ID sensors, the size of a grain of rice, which can be placed in or on almost anything that is manufactured. These sensors can send information to the Internet and onto the cloud, huge storage areas full of storage devices, which can record limitless bits of information for future retrieval.

The Cloud

The cloud, brimming with billions and soon trillions of pieces of information from almost any manufactured product, any ideas, or development of almost any line of thought, can produce data that can be used by the designer, the manufacturer, retailer, and consumer, or, perhaps more accurately stated, cyber investigators and researchers looking for information that could be of benefit to any of those interested.

For example, most cars produced today have computers on board that use sensors to send information to the cloud that can be accessed by the manufacturer to better understand the quality of the vehicle, the retailer to learn which vehicles have the longest lifespan, and the consumer who is regularly reminded of the maintenance is needed or component parts that are needing repair. Already, some car manufacturers like Tesla are able to make improvements in the car through the Internet without ever having the car brought in for maintenance.

The community college and university will be impacted by the IoT in a variety of ways. Manufacturers and retailers will need specialists who can access the data from the cloud, analyze the data, and recommend improvement needed for a better product that is more conducive to the consumer. This will demand training and licensing for the workforce. In addition, there will be currently unthought-of ways that the collected data could be used. It will inspire entrepreneurs to develop new jobs in the future that do not exist today.

Personal Robots

Robots are already an important part of manufacturing today and have been for a few decades. A machine that can do a repetitive function over and over without tiring, needing a break, or leaving the plant for sleep is greatly appreciated in the manufacturing field. However, the personal robot is another thing altogether. These robots that can be of assistance in the home, the office, the school room, and the international conference are just around the corner in terms of development.

Expect in the near future to see personal robots on a college campus in a broad spectrum of activities. If the work is repetitive, it is possible for robots to provide it. The impact on community colleges will be programs in robot repair and programming. Universities will develop new robots to meet the demands of the household and workplace. It is entirely possible that higher education in 2050 will look completely different from today. Brick and mortar facilities may have gone the way of the dinosaurs, being replaced by robots with teaching and learning conducted through the Internet.

Quantum Computing

One more technology moving to Stage 2 in the 2025–2030 time frame is quantum computing. Although the other technologies in this time frame will create serious disruptions in areas that are well understood, quantum computing is another story altogether. It is truly a game-changer. The world of the early 2020s is comfortable with the expansion of computing power guided by Moore's Law, which suggests that computer power and computer storage doubles every 18–24 months. Computer power has developed from one transistor on a chip the size of a human thumbnail in 1957 to 100 billion transistors on a chip that same size in 2019. The speed of quantum computing changes everything; Moore's Law will become a thing of the past.

The impact on higher education will be expansive. Its use in manufacturing, genome development, the mind of a robot, and the Internet is almost beyond comprehension today. And yet, it is here and it will be used, hopefully for the benefit of mankind. It provides the very real possibility of the creation of a computer mentality equal to the mind of man. It provides a pathway to go far beyond the mental capacity of humans. It could in a five-year period go from a mind with an Intelligence Quotient (IQ) of a few hundred to one with an IQ in the millions. It holds the potential to go beyond just a game-changer to a totally new game that has never existed in the history of the mankind.

The fact that the first quantum computer was developed by an American computer company is a significant happening. Whoever obtains quantum computing first will have a great advantage. It will throw classical computing out the window and replace it with computing power and storage beyond the wildest imagining. The sheer speed at which it operates will make all current cryptography obsolete overnight. It will provide the military with data that could change the notions of war completely; it will make the possibilities of deep space travel realistic, and it will have the potential to revise segments of the universe as it is known it today.

Higher education will never be the same after quantum computing becomes normal. Its impact will delve into every corner of the university and community college. In the near future, quantum computing holds potential of completely changing the methods and operation of higher education. This is a technology to monitor closely and continuously in order to make sense of it, and find ways to harness it in higher education. Either higher education learns to deal with quantum computing or it will deal with community colleges and higher education.

3D Printing

3D printing has existed for a few decades. Plentiful small models have flooded the market displaying the potential of the process. In more recent years, the time frame to print a product has decreased significantly. The ability of 3D printing has been expanded with a variety of sources including plastics, metals, and concrete. 3D printing, also known as additive manufacturing, can construct a house in a matter of days, rather than months, at costs far less than normal construction.

Additive Manufacturing Housing

If additive manufactured housing were in full operation a few years ago, the hurricane disasters that hit Puerto Rico and the Bahamas and destroyed conventional housing could have been entirely rebuilt in a matter of months. Since tornadoes also destroy housing, business structures, hospitals, and schools, additive manufacturing could shorten the time to rebuild and the costs involved in doing so. Housing is just one use for 3D printing. With a blueprint or a photo of other manufactured products, 3D printing could be used to make replacement parts in the home as easy as paper copies are printed with today's computer printers.

Impact on Higher Education

The impact of this technology will produce the need for new programs at the community college. It is also an area for further research and development at the university. The technology is well along its way in Stage 1 and headed for Stage 2 most likely in the late 2020s. Opportunities for existing businesses and start-up entrepreneurial possibilities are many. Higher education can lead the way in developing this technology if it is aware of and interested in researching and developing its possibilities. The potential benefit to higher education is tremendous.

Narrow Artificial Intelligence

Artificial intelligence has existed for some time in narrow forms. For example, when a book is purchased from Amazon, the computer keeps track of the purchase and an algorithm reviews the files for books that might be of similar interested to the consumer. It will suggest possibilities that the purchaser may want to pursue. As more books are bought, the computer algorithm searches the list of books of similar interest and will suggest more to the purchaser. Computer software that operates in that way can be of considerable assistance to the purchaser when looking for books in a particular field.

ARTIFICIAL GENERAL INTELLIGENCE

Artificial General Intelligence (AGI) is something altogether different. When computer intelligence that is equal to that of a human being is developed, it will create the possibility of AGI with the potential of a much higher IQ than that of normal human beings. According to Ray Kurzweil (2005) in his book, *The Singularity Is Near*, if computer power continues to double every two years as described by Moore's Law, there will be enough computer power to match a human brain, creating AGI by 2045 (Kurzweil, 2005).

In 2019 when Google developed its first model of a quantum computer, Kurzweil, who now works for Google, changed his forecast for the AGI from 2045 to 2030. Why could he do that? The quantum computer, which uses atoms rather than silicon chips, increases the speed of operation to truly blinding velocities.

With quantum computing, AGI could become Artificial Super Intelligence (ASI) almost immediately. It will not take a series of years; more likely it will take a few months. The existence of ASI creates great excitement, anticipation, and fear on the part of futurists. It could take over everything in a very short period of time. It is possible that mankind will be at a loss as to how to deal with it. James Barrat (2013) envisioned that fear in his book *Our Final Invention: Artificial Intelligence and the End of the Human Era*. He did it when Moore's Law was the guideline and before Google developed an early quantum computer.

Other authors take a more optimistic approach, such as Nick Bostrom (2014) in his book *Superintelligence: Paths, Dangers, Strategies*. He believes that human beings will find ways to adapt to the changes and learn to live successfully with them (Bostrom, 2014). Woodrow Barfield (2015) in *Cyber Humans: Our Future with Machines* expects that humans will become cyber-humans by having chips inserted or connected to human minds that will allow them to deal successfully with and AGI or and ASI (Barfield, 2015).

The impact on higher education is difficult to imagine. Hopefully humans will figure out how to add a chip to the human brain that will help them keep up with the robot with ASI mind. How higher education will be affected seems almost an impossible question to answer. With chips inserted or connected to the human brain, community colleges and universities as known and operating today most likely will have a very short shelf life. Adaptation will become the watchword.

Phenomenal Coming Disruptions

Community colleges and universities will experience phenomenal, continuing disruptions. The question may become, of what use are human beings? That is not a question that the human race will want to find itself having to answer. Instead, human beings will need to research, study, experiment, and innovate like never before. If operating in a way that is trying to figure out the proper place of human beings in such a rapid and extensive set of changes, higher education may be able to understand and learn how to cope with and use the changes for its benefit.

Autonomous Cars

From one perspective, it would seem that autonomous cars are a good idea. They would reduce traffic accidents and deaths, make traveling a computerized controlled process, and allow for traveling in very comfortable, safe conditions. Today there are still safety issues, insurance concerns, and a lack of regulations at the state and federal levels. Those will all have to be developed and put in place, which is the reason that Stage 2 of autonomous cars is most likely coming in the decade of the 2030s. However, this is a technology that could move to Stage 2 much sooner if the issues, concerns, and regulations were developed more rapidly.

For community colleges, current automotive programs would see a significant change. If gasoline-powered vehicles become electrically powered, additional changes in repair and maintenance will occur. Universities would see engineering programs that constantly research and develop improved methods of safety and other topics still to be developed. Another interesting change may come to NASCAR and quarter mile racing. Will a human no longer drive the car? Will robots take over that function? Horse racing is still a sport enjoyed by many people; maybe car racing will continue on as well.

Assuming that autonomous cars—gasoline powered, hybrid, or fully electric—will become the new normal in the 2030s or before, community colleges will need to provide retraining for their automotive instructors. Autonomous cars will include increased electronics, increased internal computers, and new digital methods of car operation and control. There will be some mechanical components to the autonomous automobile but they will become the smaller segment of the vehicle needing maintenance. The larger number of components will need training in electronics and computers.

The university will most likely develop programs that enhance autonomous cars, create software that help to control the car, avoid accidents, and increase safety. There may be grants awarded to universities to design military machines to fight wars autonomously. Since the autonomous car is actually a type of robot, it may have uses by the military that could completely change methods of warfare. The business community and the military may be looking to the universities to develop components and concepts that could make autonomous cars and military vehicles successful.

Bitcoin/Blockchain

This potential revolution in the financial world is operating somewhat under the radar today. It exists and is used, but nothing close to the hype and interest that was heard in the latter part of the first decade of the twenty-first century when it first appeared on the scene. What was considered to be a digital method of handling financial affairs that would literally put existing banks out of business did not happen. The idea that the process could not be hacked was put to the test when millions of dollars were stolen by a hacker. Since that time, efforts have been made to improve the process, but at present, the notion of an impenetrable system has not been fully developed.

If the issues with the digital process of handling financial and contract processes can be improved to the point where it is unhackable, then this method of dealing with financial affairs has significant potential. If the issues cannot be adequately solved, Bitcoin/Blockchain most likely will die for lack of trust by the potential users. If the issues can be solved, community colleges and senior institutions will have to make significant changes in their business and financial program offerings and courses.

Human Genome Development

As the development of human genome therapy moves to Stage 2, the impact on community colleges will be found in the addition of new programs such as those assisting a surgeon in creating the changes in the human body. Exactly what this kind of program will look like in reality remains a question at present, but assistants of various types may be needed. At the university level, research and experimentation in the human genome field will be ongoing in rapid fashion. The potential to cure medical afflictions will be sought by many at the university level.

The development of designer children could bring both grants and new programs to universities. This concept, if accepted by the population and legalized by the federal government, could create significant need for further research at the university level. The ethical issues alone could keep university law programs going for years.

Nanotechnology

Nanotechnology, the only technology forecasted to obtain Stage 2 in 2040–2045, has as much potential to change the world as quantum computing or Artificial General Intelligence. It, too, is a game-changer in the truest meaning of that phrase. It allows finished products to be constructed from atoms. As such, it could make 3D printing look like a primitive tool. Nanotechnology needs no steel, copper, plastic, wood, silicon, or anything else that is used to create products today. The country using it to make salable products only needs access to atoms, highly trained scientists to operate the processes, appropriate equipment, and a workable environment. It allows any country that can use the process to be truly self-sustaining.

For that matter, it allows for anything to be made anywhere here on Earth, its moon, other planets in the solar system, the galaxy, or any other galaxy that is made up of atoms. The raw material is the atom itself which, in the universe, apparently exists almost everywhere. With nanotechnology, robots, spaceships, clothing, housing, vehicles, and so on could be constructed. This is truly an amazing game-changer.

Its impact on higher education is phenomenal. It poses no limits on what can be made from atoms. It is unbelievable, but real. Already there has been considerable research and development of this technology. It is extremely complex because atoms reside in the quantum world, which operates under totally different laws than the visible world. Higher education will look very different in a world with nanotechnology. Learning how to use it, repair it, maintain it, and experiment with it will most likely take years.

TEN TECHNOLOGIES AND THE FUTURE

Seven of the technologies, agricultural genome development, Internet of Things, personal robots, 3D printing, autonomous cars, Bitcoin/Blockchain, and human genome development, are relatively easy to understand conceptually. They bring disruptive changes to the current world, but they appear to bring positive results that can benefit mankind. The chances of adapting to them and using them seem possible, disruptive as they may be.

Three Big Elephants in the Room

The other three, quantum computing, Artificial General Intelligence, and nanotechnology are, each in their own way, game-changers. They are not easy to adapt to and will take considerable effort to control. In the case of Artificial General Intelligence, it literally has a mind of its own. No one at present is sure whether the AGI, let alone the ASI, mentality can be controlled for the benefit of mankind. ASI may take off pursuing goals of its own making. Further, as these three technologies combine with each other and/or some of the seven other technologies, some totally unexpected and unforeseen things are likely to occur.

Quantum computing will speed up the development of all the technologies. Artificial General Intelligence and its descendant Artificial Super Intelligence have the potential to disrupt and interfere with the way mankind currently interacts with itself, the world, the solar system, galaxy, and the universe itself. Nanotechnology opens the doors of creation to mankind. Combine quantum computing or nanotechnology with AGI and ASI and overnight the human race could find itself in great trouble or unimagined benefit.

CONCLUSION

The generations of mankind who follow the current ones to the end of the twenty-first century will observe, live through, understand, and hopefully, construct a beneficial future world for all concerned that is far beyond the current ability to envision. Higher education will become something totally different than it is today. Just what that will be is hard to imagine.

CHAPTER 3 SUMMARY

- Each of the ten technologies discussed earlier in this book will create disruptions in higher education as they move to Stage 2, exponential development.
- Dr. Jennifer Doudna describes the scientific journey she and a fellow scientist Dr. Emmanuelle Charpentier traveled to determine how genes could be moved, deleted, and added using a process called CRISPR/Cas9.
- The potential for developing cures is tremendous.
- When Doudna finished her work on genes, she got worried that maybe she had done the wrong thing as the information could be used for both positive and negative purposes.
- In animal husbandry, finding ways to alter the gene structure is not a new idea as it has been done for centuries by mating the strongest and best farm animals for better results.
- With CRISPR/Cas9, ideas, experiments, and results happen much faster and with less guesswork.
- The impact on universities is tremendous as the need for agricultural scientists will increase significantly.
- The impact on community colleges may very well create a resumption of agricultural programs that have for the most part been removed from offerings for a lack of student interest and farming needs.
- Farms operated in a digital manner may lead to vertical farming.
- Vertical farming is the practice of producing food indoors, on vertically inclined surfaces.
- Vertical farming provides control of the weather as the entire process takes place indoors.
- Vertical farming does not use soil as the growing medium as on a normal farm.

- Instead, it uses aeroponic, aquaponics, or hydroponic mediums for the growing medium.
- Vertical farming could take place close to metropolitan areas, which would reduce the costs transportation of food from farm to market.
- The IoT works by using radio frequency ID sensors, the size of a grain of rice that can be placed in or on almost anything that is manufactured.
- The clouds, brimming with billions and soon trillions of pieces of information from almost any manufactured product, can produce data that can be used by the designer, the manufacturer, retailer, and consumer.
- Some car manufacturers like Tesla are able to make improvements in the car through the Internet without ever having the car brought in for maintenance.
- Currently unthought-of ways that the data collected could be used.
- It will inspire entrepreneurs to develop new jobs in the future that do not exist today.
- Personal robots that can be of assistance in the home or the office, the school room, or the international conference are just around the corner in terms of development.
- If the work is repetitive, it is possible for robots to provide it.
- It is entirely possible that higher education in 2050 will look completely different from today.
- Brick and mortar facilities may be replaced by robots teaching and learning through the Internet.
- The last of the technologies moving to Stage 2 in the 2025–2030 time frame is quantum computing, truly a game-changer.
- The results of Moore's Law in the transistor world are well known.
- The speed at which quantum computing operates created by the atoms that power it reach out toward infinity.
- Quantum computing provides a pathway to go far beyond the mental capacity of humans.
- It could, in a five-year period, develop a mentality with an Intelligence Quotient (IQ) of a few hundred to one with an IQ of millions.
- Whoever obtains quantum computing first will have a great advantage.

- It will throw classical computing out the window and replace it with computing power and storage beyond the wildest imagining.
- Higher education will never be the same after quantum computing becomes normal.
- Its impact will delve into every corner of the university and community college.
- Either higher education learns to deal with quantum computing or it will deal with community colleges and higher education.
- 3D printing, also known as additive manufacturing, can construct a house in a matter of days rather than months, costs far less than normal construction, and is constructed with walls that are strong enough to handle hurricane-force winds.
- Since tornadoes also destroy housing, business structures, hospitals, and schools, additive manufacturing could shorten the time to rebuild and the costs involved in doing so.
- The impact of this technology will produce the need for new programs at the community college and area for further research and development at the university.
- Artificial intelligence has existed for some time in narrow forms.
- According to futurist Ray Kurzweil, if computer power continues to double every two years as described by Moore's Law, there will be enough computer power to match a human brain, creating Artificial General Intelligence by 2045.
- When Google developed its first model of a quantum computer, Kurzweil changed his forecast for the creation of an Artificial General Intelligence from 2045 to 2030.
- The existence of ASI creates great excitement, anticipation, and fear on the part of futurists as it could take over everything in a very short period of time.
- Quantum computing is many multiple times faster than computing using silicon chips.
- Add ASI to a robot brain or many robot brains and the world as it is known today changes exponentially and beyond.
- The impact on higher education is difficult to imagine.
- Hopefully humans will figure out how to add a chip to the brain that will help them keep up with the robot with ASI.

- Where does that leave higher education?
- Community colleges and universities will see phenomenal, continuing disruptions.
- Higher education, if operating in a way that is trying to figure out the proper place of human beings in such a rapid and extensive set of disruptions, may be able to understand and learn how to cope and use the changes for its benefit.
- From one perspective, it would seem that autonomous cars are a good idea.
- They would reduce traffic accidents and deaths, make traveling a computerized controlled process, and allow for traveling in very comfortable conditions.
- For community colleges, current automotive programs would see a significant change.
- Will a human no longer drive the car?
- Will robots take over that function?
- Assuming that autonomous cars, gasoline-powered, hybrid, or fully electric, will become the new normal in the 2030s or before, community colleges will need to retrain their automotive instructors.
- The university will most likely develop programs that enhance autonomous cars, create software that help to control the car, avoid accidents, and increase safety.
- Bitcoin/Blockchain has the potential to create a revolution in the financial world, but is operating somewhat under the radar today.
- If the issues cannot be adequately solved, the method most likely will die because of lack of trust by the potential users.
- In the human genome arena, as the development of genome therapy moves to Stage 2, the impact on community colleges will be found in the addition of new programs such as those assisting a surgeon in creating the changes in the human body.
- The development of designer children could bring both grants and new programs to the university.
- This concept, if accepted by the population and legalized by the federal government, could create significant need for further research at the university level.

- Nanotechnology, the only technology forecasted to reach Stage 2 in 2040–2045, has as much potential to change the world as quantum computing.
- Nanotechnology needs no steel, copper, plastic, wood, silicon, or anything else that is used to create products today.
- It allows any country that can use the process to be truly self-sustaining.
- With nanotechnology robots, spaceships, clothing, housing, vehicles, and so on could be constructed anywhere in the universe that atoms exist.
- Higher education will look very different in a world with nanotechnology.
- Seven of the technologies, agricultural genome development, the Internet of Things, personal robots, 3D printing, autonomous cars, Bitcoin/Blockchain, and human genome development, bring disruptive changes to the current world, but they appear to bring positive results that can benefit mankind.
- Quantum computing, Artificial General Intelligence, and nanotechnology are, each in their own way, game-changers.
- No one at present is sure whether the AGI, let alone the ASI, mentality can be controlled for the benefit of mankind.

Chapter Four

Mission and Vision

Each institution of higher education from community college to university must develop its mission and vision. The mission clearly states the purpose of the institution. It answers the question of why it exists. The vision describes the general direction of the institution, given its location, student body, business community, and the economic development organizations, which are local for a community college and much broader for a university. These two critical concepts, when properly developed, give clear foundational structure to the institution.

Given the technological world that the institutions of higher education face, what is an appropriate method for developing the mission and vision? Since the future is where the graduates from the institutions will live and work, it is critical that the mission and vision be carefully crafted for the benefit of those leading, teaching, and staffing the institution that provides the gateway to successful future careers for graduates. The mission and vision provide the foundation to build upon and can be best completed using a data-driven method.

MISSION

When a new president is hired at an institution of higher education, he or she often begins with an in-depth investigation of the mission. Is it viable as is or does it needs modification? Sometimes the new president is interested in making some changes. The standard process is to work with faculty, staff, administrators, community leaders, business CEOs, and economic development leaders to determine the answer to that question and take appropriate action. As a twentieth-century model, that method has worked quite well.

However, in the twenty-first century, with potential disruptions about to impact the institutions in periodically, more must be done. There needs to be research into whether any of the ten technologies described earlier in this book are going to specifically impact the institution. It will take an investigation into how far the technologies are along the Stage 1 pathway, when they move to Stage 2, and how might they disrupt the institution as currently configured. The committee should be made up of members of the faculty, staff, administration, students, community leaders, business CEOs, and economic development officials.

The Mission/Vision Committee

The Mission/Vision Committee should research the technologies as they pertain to the local school systems, future educational and training needs of the business community, health community, and economic development organizations. To begin with, the committee needs to determine which of the ten technologies will impact the institution. With that important consideration completed, the committee is ready to move ahead.

In the twenty-first century, the mission should be developed in a general way that determines what the future holds for the students after graduation and what kind of training and education they will need to be successful in the future. The mission should be dynamic, prepared for constant change, and written in such a way as to demonstrate the institution is open to making modifications in its concepts to meet the technological disruptions as they appear. Reports and presentations from this committee should be prepared for discussion with the leadership of the institution.

When the committee has completed research, written the reports, and made presentations, the Mission/Vision Committee in concert with the president and administrators will determine the final wording of the mission statement to be presented to the board for approval. It is critically important that the mission reflects the purpose of the institution to meet current and future needs as determined by the collection of research data. Creating or revising the mission will take some time, anywhere from three to six months.

VISION

Once the mission is approved by the board, it is time to develop the vision for the institution. The Mission/Vision Committee should take its report on the technologies and discuss the need for further research with all of the technologies that are expected to impact the institution. The committee should try to look into the future as far as possible to determine the general direction of the college over the next ten years.

Future-Back Thinking

Assistance in developing the vision is a process outlined in *Lead from the Future: How to Turn Visionary Thinking into Breakthrough Growth* (Johnson and Suskewicz, 2020). The notion of "future-back thinking and planning" is an excellent way of preparing for the vision. (Johnson and Suskewicz, 2020, p. 10). These authors contend that creating a vision for an organization is an important initial step when creating a plan for the organization.

Present-Forward Thinking

They point out that planning in the business world and other organizations work usually from "present-forward" thinking that is supported with information from the past successes and failures of the organization. They contend a much more advantageous way to develop the vision is to use "future-back" thinking (Johnson & Suskewicz, 2020, p. 10). "Present-Forward thinking is driven by known facts, and data; future-back thinking is low in initial knowledge and high in assumptions—its aim is to discover what could be true" (Johnson & Suskewicz, 2020, p. 44). Their suggested method is to bring together a group such as the Mission/Vision Committee within the organization who would have in-depth conversations on what the organization could look like in ten years or more in the future.

The members of the committee would prepare themselves by reading extensively what is currently being said about envisioning what a successful organization would look like in the future, some ten years or more out. In addition to the mission of the organization, using a future-back method of determining the vision can create a general direction(s) that could be accepted across the board in terms of faculty, staff, board members, and external stakeholders. That kind of vision would become the foundation for goal setting over a one to two-year period and objectives over a matter of months or weeks. It would provide a future direction that could be pursued by strategic planning and short-term action steps.

The idea is not to create a predestined future for the institution of higher education, but rather to have some say in actually developing what is to come (Johnson & Suskewicz, 2020, p. 216). The Mission/Vision Committee should develop an open-ended vision statement, based on the best future-back thinking. It should allow for periodic changes as needed. The vision for the institution should be flexible, adaptable, and as accurate as possible, given the chances for disruptions that the ten technologies may create for the institution.

The Future Pathway

The vision needs to provide a broad, easily modified sketch of the future pathway of the institution. Specifics will come later in the strategic planning process as described in a later chapter. Both the mission and vision statements should be crafted as briefly as possible. Both should be easily read and repeated, if at all possible. These two documents are to be published widely internally and externally. They provide the foundation of the strategic planning process to come. Careful, accurate crafting of the vision is critical for the future success of the institution.

CONCLUSION

Developing an accurate mission and future-focused vision allows all stakeholders to fully understand the purpose of the institution and its general direction(s) into the future. Revising the mission and vision as described will allow for continuous, dynamic planning.

CHAPTER 4 SUMMARY

- Every institution of higher education from community college to university must develop its mission and vision.
- These two critical concepts, when developed, give clear foundational structure to the institution.
- Since the future is where the graduates from the institutions will live and work, it is critical that the mission and vision be carefully crafted for the benefit of those leading, teaching, and staffing the institution that provides the gateway to successful careers for graduates.
- Often when a new president is hired at an institution of higher education, he or she often begins with an in-depth investigation of the mission.
- There needs to be research into whether any of the ten technologies described earlier in this book are going to specifically impact the institution.
- The Mission/Vision Committee should research the technologies as they pertain to the local school systems, future needs of the business community, health community, and economic development agencies.
- The mission should be dynamic, open to constant changes, and written in such a way as to demonstrate the institution is open to making modifications in its concepts to meet the technological disruptions as they appear.
- It is critically important that the mission reflects not only the purpose of the institution to meet current needs, but also to meet the future needs as determined by the research data.

- The Mission/Vision Committee should be developed made up of a cross-section of stakeholders.
- With sufficient data collected, the committee should try to look into the future as far as possible to determine the general direction of the college over the next ten years or more.
- Assistance in developing the vision is a concept described by Mark Johnson and Josh Suskewicz (2020) in their book, *Lead from the Future: How to Turn Visionary Thinking into Breakthrough Growth*.
- Their concept is to bring together groups within the organization that would have in-depth conversations on what the organization could look like in ten years or more in the future.
- The groups would prepare themselves by reading extensively on what is currently being said about the future and then envisioning what a successful organization would look like in that environment.
- The idea of thinking ahead in time, envisioning what higher education will be ten or more years ahead, and then using that vision to set the general direction of the community college or university makes all kinds of sense.
- The idea is not to create a predestined future for the institution of higher education, but rather to have some say in actually developing what is to come.
- The vision for the institution should be flexible, adaptable, and as accurate as possible, given the chances for disruptions that the ten technologies may create for the institution.
- The vision needs to provide a broad, easily modified sketch of the future pathway of the institution.
- Developing an accurate mission and future-focused vision allows all stakeholders to fully understand the purpose of the institution and its general direction(s) into the future.

Chapter Five

ARPAC

A Strategic Planning Process

After mission and vision statements are completed, it is time to develop the strategic plan for the institution. Strategic planning outside of the military harks back to the 1960s with Robert McNamara who served under Presidents Kennedy and Johnson as Secretary of Defense. McNamara developed a strategic planning system for the government that was quickly picked up by business and industry. It actually worked reasonably well if it was used in a business that had control of the raw materials, manufacturing process, personnel, and sales. The all-under-one-roof planning process worked because by far most of the variables were under the control of the business.

NEW PLANNING MODEL NEEDED

In the twenty-first century, with potential technological changes impacting higher education from a number of directions, the planning method used by most organizations is no longer working as well as it had earlier. Higher education, along with the business community, is in need of a different kind of planning process, one that is continuous, dynamic, and future-focused. This chapter will outline a method that will support the need for a revised planning process for higher education in particular.

The planning process described in this book is strategic in that it is made up of the vision direction(s), long-range planning goals, and short-term planning objectives. In a serially disruptive environment, such as will be experienced in the twenty-first century, setting goals in a five to ten-year time frame is not enough and further, will not work successfully. Rather, the planning should begin with a vision of ten years in the future or more, followed by the goals in the two-to-three-year time frame that are subject to change or replacement as needed. When moving toward the goals, short-term objectives should be specific for completion in weeks or months. The objectives should lead in the direction of the goals and the vision but be open to change as each objective is being pursued.

Nine of the ten technologies described earlier are predicted to move to the exponential Stage 2 within less than a decade and a half, with each of them bringing disruptions to current methods of operation. It is critical that a new method of planning be used; a plan that operates in a continuous, dynamic way. The ARPAC Model provides such a process.

THE ARPAC MODEL

The ARPAC Model is made up of five steps: Awareness, Research, Planning, Action, and Caring, each described separately in the following chapters (Staat, 2019). The process was developed to help higher education institutions accurately plan their future directions given the ten technologies that will impact the institutions with serial disruptions. The impacts will come periodically, rather than arriving all at once. Having a method to prepare for and deal successfully with each of those disruptions as they arrive is the focus of the process.

To help make the process clear, the following chapters of the book will discuss the process step-by-step. The process changes planning from developing a set of goals and objectives set in stone for an upcoming number of years into a continuous planning process that begins with a vision and dynamically moves from point to point while simultaneously being open to making modifications where and when needed.

This book started with an analogy of sliding down a chute on a toboggan. How does that enjoyable activity give insight into how the ARPAC process works? First, the people going down the hill intertwine themselves for the ride; it is a team effort. Second, the trip from the top to the bottom of the hill is fast with everyone hanging on for dear life. No one can drag his or her foot along; everyone is focused on getting down the ride in a successful manner. Third, the ride is repetitious. Once to the bottom, everyone untangles themselves and holds onto the rope while walking back to the top of the hill. It is a continuous, repetitive process that causes the team on the toboggan to be successful each time they slide down the hill.

Toboggan theory can be assisted by a parallel dynamic planning process initiated by computer software designers called Scrum. That term comes from the way rugby is played with a team trying to control a football while walking, running, passing, and sometimes crawling down the field. When they get stopped, they regroup and attempt to move the ball down field again. The process is continuous and repetitious toward meeting the objective of getting to the goal.

Use of the Scrum Process

The Scrum process made sense to software developers. They started with a goal in mind and worked through a series of objectives to accomplish it. When they produced a final product which they know that, although it may be salable, will need changes in the near future due to a variety of issues with the software itself and to changes in needs from the consumer. The designers know the software is, in fact, never finished, but is always in need of further development (Sutherland & Sutherland, 2014). They, like the rugby players, repeat the process over and over. They, like the toboggan riders, make rapid trips to the bottom of the issue and return preparing for the next revision that will have to be made.

Both the toboggan theory and the Scrum process drive provide excellent examples of the continuous, repetitious method that ARPAC uses. Planning moves from a static process to a dynamic one because each the ten technologies may disrupt whatever the plan is. It will then have to be modified to deal with issues that were not foreseen. In the world of higher education those issues may directly cause immediate changes in current programs and/or require the rapid development of entirely new programs. To best serve the student, programs must be not only up to date, but also designed to change at a moment's notice to meet dynamic needs.

CONCLUSION

The five parts of the ARPAC process will guide the institution of higher education. It will provide data and information to help the administrators, faculty, staff, students, the business community, and economic development agencies understand what is at stake. Beyond a basic understanding, the results of research will provide data that expands the understanding, which leads to the development of planning, action, and caring.

CHAPTER 5 SUMMARY

- After mission and vision statements are completed, it is time to develop the strategic plan for the institution.
- Robert McNamara developed a strategic planning system for the government that was quickly picked up by business and industry.
- The planning process described in this book is strategic in that it is made up long-range planning goals combined with short-term planning objectives.
- The process was developed to help higher education institutions accurately plan their future directions given the ten technologies that will impact the institutions with serial disruptions.
- The process changes planning from developing set of goals and objectives set in stone for an upcoming number of years into a continuous planning process that dynamically moves from point to point.

- This book started with an analogy of sliding down a chute on a toboggan, which gives insight into how the ARPAC process works.
- It is a continuous, repetitive process that causes the team on the toboggan to be successful each time it slides down the hill.
- The Scrum process made sense to software developers.
- They started with a goal in mind and worked through a series of objectives to accomplish it.
- The designers know the software is in fact never finished, but is always in need of further development.
- They, like rugby players, repeat the process over and over.
- They, like the toboggan riders, make rapid trips to the bottom of the issue and return preparing for the next revision that will have to be made.
- Planning moves from a static process to a dynamic one because the ten technologies may disrupt whatever the plan is, which will then have to be modified to deal with issues that were not foreseen.
- The five parts of the ARPAC process will guide the institution of higher education.

Chapter Six

ARPAC Step 1

Awareness

Leaders in higher education need to be aware of the ten technologies that are now developing in the twenty-first century. They need to know that the linear development stage of a technology is followed by the exponential stage. It will be critical that the leaders in community colleges and universities understand when and how the technology could impact the institution. Changes may need to be made in short order to keep the institution viable and successful for students, the business community, and economic development. It is critical that the institution be ready to adapt to what is coming.

UNDERSTANDING THE DIGITAL WORLD

Some might argue that institutions of higher education have always been aware of and adapting to potential changes. However, in the twenty-first century, the exponential velocity at which the technologies will develop in Stage 2 will require considerably more attention than those that developed in a linear manner, as in the twentieth century. The digital world of the twenty-first century will most likely appear as confusing, complicated, and continuously disruptive. Higher education leaders, including presidents, vice presidents, deans, department heads, and faculty will need to be re-educated. It is important to remember the extremely rapid speed at which Uber, Airbnb, and Amazon developed.

All three of those organizations grew at exponential speeds that surprised the competition with methods to deliver services that had not been thought of before. Taxis had been in existence for centuries before Uber appeared on the scene. Bed and breakfast homes were spread throughout the United States and beyond for decades. Retail businesses date but to early human history. Then suddenly, out of nowhere, three new ideas become realities in a matter of a few years. Further, all three impacted the status quo with totally unexpected force. The few who saw the change coming had the opportunity to adapt quickly. Most others were surprised and not sure how to adapt.

So far, in terms of higher education, the only unexpected competition have come from online courses and MOOCs. Neither of them have become competitive enough to undermine the way things are being done; however, unconsidered possibilities may exist in development behind the scenes. With little or no warning they could appear and create considerable disruptions.

Even if new and creative approaches to learning do not appear, the ten technologies will reach Stage 2 at some point. They will impact community colleges and universities in unexpected ways that could shake the foundations of the institutions, if they are not prepared to deal with them. There is a definite need for a re-education of those who lead, teach, and staff higher education in order to make certain that the impacts are become incorporated into the institutions or at the very least, dealt with in a positive manner.

Re-education Needed

The re-education should be founded in growth mindset. According to Dr. Carol Dweck of Stanford University, in her book *Mindset: The New Psychology of Success*, a growth mindset is defined as being open to change, willing grow with change, and developing ways to deal with it (Dweck, 2006). A growth mindset will be critical to success for future community college and university leaders, faculty, staff, and students.

A mindset that is constantly future-focused and able to adapt to the serial disruptions that twenty-first-century technologies will bring will make success possible.

THE FIVE-STEP PROCESS

Success can be accomplished by using a five-step process: Awareness, Research, Planning, Action, and Caring (ARPAC), all of which have a foundation in a growth mindset. For success, the entire process must be used continuously as technologies develop exponentially and create serial disruptions that will affect higher education. Adapting rapidly will make all the difference between those institutions who are able to change their ways and those who cannot, or those who choose the status quo, and those who will not.

In addition to all the other issues such as recruitment, retention, funding, facilities, equipment, and the like, leaders in higher education need to become aware of the ten technologies that are developing in the twenty-first century. They need to understand that the linear development phase of a technology is followed by the exponential phase. The potential impact on the institution of each of the ten technologies will need to be thoroughly analyzed. It will be critical that the leaders in every community college and university understand when and how the technology could impact their respective institutions.

Recently, higher education was impacted by a digital teaching method called Massive Open Online Course (MOOC). It did not strike community colleges and universities extremely hard, but it was an attempt to completely upend higher education. MOOCs most likely will not totally disappear, but even though they did not cause higher education to be significantly revised, it should be remembered as a warning. There are possibilities on the fringes that may create even larger impacts in the future. Online education is another real possibility as was demonstrated in its use in reaction to the COVID-19 pandemic.

Awareness: Step 1

Awareness is the first step in dealing with the ten technologies that exist and are developing toward Stage 2. When that second stage is attained, rapid accelerating change will invade the halls, classrooms, and labs of higher education. Knowing the technologies exist and are developing in Stage 1 is critical to the future success of community colleges and universities nationally. How is awareness obtained that will keep institutions of higher education fully informed of development of the ten technologies?

There are many books that deal with the subject such as *The Fourth Industrial Revolution* by Klaus Schwab (2016). Others include *The Second Machine Age* by Erik Brynjolfsson and Andrew McAfee (2014), *The Inevitable: Understanding the 12 Technological Forces that Will Shape Our Future* by Kevin Kelly (2016), *Facing an Exponential Future: Technology and the Community College* by Darrel Staat (2018), or *Thank you for Being Late: An Optimist's Guide to Thriving in the Age of Accelerations* by Thomas Friedman (2016).

These and many other books will provide the insight needed to become aware of what technologies are out there currently under development. These volumes bring awareness that will begin to impress on all concerned the critical importance of what is heading toward higher education. In addition, probing the Internet under the heading of each technology will provide significant amounts of information.

The Awareness Requirement

Being aware of what exists and how it might impact higher education is a critical first step in the ARPAC process. It is easy to dismiss the development of the ten technologies as they are for the most part working through their designs in the background. In the twentieth century higher education could wait and see what the final product is and decide what to do about it then; however, in the twenty-first century to wait and see is to invite calamity.

CONCLUSION

Awareness is the watchword that begins the journey toward future possibilities. Those who are aware have the best chance at keeping their institutions successful for all concerned. It is a requirement of leaders in higher education, otherwise they will have no excuse for guiding the community colleges and universities in unsuccessful directions. Making certain that the awareness is developed fully will include the information in the next chapter, which will discuss Step 2, research.

CHAPTER 6 SUMMARY

- It is critical to be ready to adapt to what is coming.
- In the twenty-first century, the exponential velocity at which the technologies will develop in Stage 2 will require considerably more attention than those that developed in a linear manner, as in the twentieth century.
- It is important to remember Uber, Airbnb, and Amazon and the speed at which they developed.
- So far, in terms of higher education the only real competition has come from online courses and MOOCs.
- Even if new and creative approaches to learning do not appear, the ten technologies will reach Stage 2 and impact community colleges and universities in unexpected ways that could shake the foundations of the institutions.
- A growth mindset will be critical to success for future community college and university leaders, faculty, staff, and students.
- Success can be accomplished by using a five-step method: Awareness, Research, Planning, Action, and Caring (ARPAC), all of which have a foundation in a growth mindset.
- The potential impact on the institution of each of the ten technologies will need to be thoroughly analyzed.
- Recently, higher education was impacted by a digital teaching method called Massive Open Online Course (MOOC).
- It did not strike community colleges and universities extremely hard, but it was an attempt to completely change higher education.

- Online education is another real possibility as was demonstrated in the educational reaction to the COVID-19 pandemic.
- Awareness is the first step in dealing with the ten technologies that exist and are developing toward Stage 2.
- How is awareness obtained that will keep institutions of higher education fully informed of development of the ten technologies?
- There are many books that deal with the subject.
- Being aware of what exists and how it might impact higher education is a critical first step in the ARPAC process.
- Awareness is the watchword that begins the journey toward future possibilities.
- Making certain that the awareness is developed fully will include the information in the next chapter, which will discuss Step 2, research.

Chapter Seven

ARPAC Step 2

Research

How does a business, health organization, economic development agency, or higher education keep up with the Stage 1 development of each of the ten twenty-first-century technologies? It is most accurately done through research, something universities have done for decades, but community colleges, on the other hand, with a focus on teaching, have done less. The largest amount of research in the community college environment has often been done in reaction to accrediting agency requirements. The need for research into the ten technologies is an important change for the community college.

IMPACT ON COMMUNITY COLLEGES

It almost goes without saying that requiring community colleges to do serious, extensive research into the development of the ten technologies will not be received with immediate acceptance. Rather, research will be considered a process most faculty and staff would like to shy away from as they do not see it as a requirement in an institution focused on teaching.

Reaction to Research Needs

As a result, training and re-education will be needed to help faculty and staff to understand the importance of doing research. Some may see it as enhancement to their particular discipline, such as those teaching in medical, business, or technical programs. Others may see research as a hassle that takes time and effort away from other functions viewed as more important. Whatever the initial reaction, the leaders of the community college will have to find ways to convince the faculty and staff of the critical importance of research into the development of the technologies that will impact their institution.

Further, research will become very important to each program at the college to keep it viable for the student, the community, and the business community. For example, when most or almost all cars become autonomous in the next decade, the teaching field and the workforce needs will see tremendous changes. Faculty teaching in that department will need to be aware of the changes in order to revise the program. Counselors will need to updated in order to properly advise students, and students will need to be aware as they prepare to enter the workforce.

Every technical, health, computer, and business program will need to have a future-focused attitude as they may be impacted by one or more of the ten technologies. Programs in the humanities will need to know what to teach students about the technologies that will be important to them in their future careers. As the technologies move from Stage 1 to Stage 2, the results of research will make certain that those programs impacted at the community college will continue to be effective in an exponential era.

IMPACT ON UNIVERSITIES

University faculty and staff may find the need for research a more reasonable requirement in that the senior institutions already require significant research for professors in their disciplines move to the associate level, tenure, and full professor level. Whatever the case, research into the development of the ten technologies will be necessary for future success. The university, faculty, staff, and students will benefit as well as the business and health workforce communities.

THE MISSION/VISION COMMITTEE

To begin, the institution should use the Mission/Vision Committee which has already looked into all ten of the technologies to see which of them have the potential of impacting programs of study, students, and the business community. (See chapter 4.) The conclusions of this committee are critically important as the identification of the technologies that are expected to affect the institution will create the need for specific committees to be set up to further research the technologies involved.

Technology Research Committees

Following the identification of the technologies that will impact the institution, Technology Research Committees should be set up to research the development of specific technologies. Each of the identified technologies should have a committee researching its Stage 1 development and the potential time frame in which each will move to Stage 2. There will be a demand for continual, ongoing research of the status of each of the existing technologies in order to determine when and how it will impact the institution and the specific program.

Agile Software Development

In the early 1990s, software developers found that the traditional methods of planning did not work well for the development of software. That led to a planning process which set a long-range goal for the development of a software. Those involved knew from the beginning that it would not meet some needs by the time the software was completed. To deal with this situation, they developed a series of steps leading toward the goal that were open ended. Further, they developed the software so that when one phase was completed, it became the foundation for the next phase, which might be significantly changed because of what was learned in phase one. That process became known as Agile.

Sequential Objectives

Even when the ultimate goal was set, it was recognized that the pathway reaching it would often need to be modified, sometimes in minor and other times major ways. The developers worked phase by phase toward the goal, making changes to solve issues as they appeared, rather than waiting til the end. Often changes in objectives could require modification in the goal. Those changes might come from internal work by the developers or externally from the businesses whose needs changed during the development process.

Short-Term Segments

Each of the phases were developed in short time frame segments so that the changes in needs of the consumer or the issues determined by the developers could be integrated into the software before starting the next phase. The software developers repeated this process phase by phase over a time period that allowed for a software to be developed that met the current needs of the business community. The developers understood that most likely there would be no end to the need for further modifications; so, even when the product was operational and salable, it had been created in an open-ended fashion so that continuous upgrades could be made as needed.

Dynamic Planning

The result was that they developed a continuous, dynamic, phase-by-phase process that ultimately met the latest needs of the business community. Further, under the leadership of Jeff Sutherland, who was interested in speeding up the process, they created a change in the Agile process known as Scrum (Sutherland & Sutherland, 2014). "The term comes from the game of rugby, and it refers to the way a team works together to move the ball down the field. Careful alignment, unity of purpose, and clarity of goal come together" (Sutherland & Sutherland,

2014, p. 8). As Sutherland further explains, "Scrum works by setting sequential goals that must be met in a fixed length of time" (Sutherland & Sutherland, 2014, p. 14).

Scrum Method in Higher Education

The Scrum method can be used to develop a research process that is continuous, dynamic, and open ended. It would provide a pathway to make appropriate plans in an exponential, disruptive, digital environment. With some minor changes the Scrum process could be a valuable tool for use in higher education. The committee would research a specific technology to discover: (1) where it is in its development within Stage 1, (2) when does it have the potential to move to Stage 2, and (3) what specific impact(s) is it likely to have on the institution? (Sutherland & Sutherland, 2014).

Next, the committee would decide what needs to be done to reach the goal. A list of what must be researched is determined, prioritized, and put in writing by the committee. The committee then develops the first research cycle, known in Scrum as a "Sprint" (Sutherland & Sutherland, 2014, p. 14). The committee decides on how much work they can complete in a set time frame. The work is divided up among the committee members and they go off to work on a specific objective, in a Sprint.

Scrum Process

Rather than let the process go on for a lengthy period, the Scrum process requires the committee to have its Sprints completed in two weeks. In addition, during the two-week period, the committee meets for one or more times in 10–15 minute stand-up meetings to assess where they are in the research process. At that short meeting each member of the committee responds to three questions: (1) What did you do since the last time we met? (2) What are you going to do before we meet again? What obstacles are getting in your way? (Sutherland & Sutherland, 2014). At the end of the two week Sprint, the entire committee meets together to determine what they have accomplished so far, what additional needs have come up, and what problems need to be resolved.

Sequential Sprints

With the first Sprint completed, the committee is ready to determine the work on the next objective to move toward the goal. The committee decides which committee members will work on which parts of the objective and sets the next time frame of two weeks. The members then work on their respective objectives and meet once or twice for a 10–15 minute stand-up meeting. In two weeks they make an assessment of progress of the Sprint and determine of the next objective. The entire process repeats until the goal is reached. One of the great advantages of this process is that it can make changes as the process goes along. That opportunity may be of inestimable value for the final output.

It is critical that each committee delve as deeply as possible into the development of the technology in order to fully understand its location in Stage 1 and it potential for disruption when it obtains Stage 2. The committee should make every effort to accurately estimate how the Stage 2 development will impact programs within the higher education institution, the service area of the institution, and the economic development potential for the area served.

The research will place the higher education institution at the forefront of what is happening with each specific technology, and allow it to provide information and data to its students, the business community, and the economic development organization, all of which will provide success for the community at large.

Examination and Analysis Committee

When the goal is reached, a report is written and the Research Committee makes a presentation to the Examination & Analysis (E&I) Committee. The committee will hear the presentation, review the report, and accept it or send it back to the committee involved for more research. Sending the report back to the Research Committee should seldom happen as the committee involved will have done its research work well. When the research committee's report is accepted, the E&I Committee will forward it to the president.

The Scrum process will help to produce more work in less time. It will be of considerable value to the institution when Stage 2 of the technology comes to fruition. The institution, rather than being caught off guard or surprised by the unexpected, will have solid research data upon which to make decisions that will lead it to viable success. This process is critically useful in an exponential planning environment when time is of the essence and action must be taken rapidly. The process provides accurate data-driven decision making that is very valuable to rapid, future-focused planning generated by the accurate research created by the committee involved.

Multiple Research Committees

If the institution of higher education has a number of research committees working on the development of more than one of the ten technologies that have potential to impact its operation and future, it will have a much better chance of keeping the institution viable and useful on more than one front to all concerned internally and externally. Reports from the committees will need to be distributed through internal websites and the institution's external website. The findings will be of interest to administrators, faculty, staff, and students internally as well as the business community, health organizations, and agencies of economic development.

The committee(s) should make every effort to accurately estimate when and how the Stage 2 development will impact programs within the higher education institution. Each research committee should distribute its findings through the use of an internal website accessible by faculty, staff, students, and administration. Beyond that, the president should call periodic meetings of administrators, faculty, staff, and student leaders at which each committee makes presentations on the findings of their respective committees. Further, information should be distributed through the institution's website to all concerned in the service area of the community college or university.

Periodic internal meetings with the institution's leadership, faculty, and staff will become critical to keep everyone knowledgeable of when and how a specific technology is expected to impact the institution. If employees at all levels in the community college are kept up to date with the findings of the research, rapid changes can be made more reasonably to serve the needs of the institution, faculty, staff, students, the local business community, local economic development agencies, and all other constituents served.

BUSINESS AND RESEARCH

It is important to remember that the business community is following the development of technologies that could help them increase production, quality, and profits. Business leaders are aware that the Stage 2 changes in a technology could benefit them significantly and they will want to investigate and integrate them as quickly as possible. The leaders know that their competition is watching the technologies as well and if they want to remain competitive in a global economy, they have no choice but to assimilate the technologies into their business practices.

Further, as the technologies become available, the businesses will be looking to community colleges and universities to provide training for the workforce, management, and others on how to best utilize the technologies that apply to each of them. Higher education institutions will need to be at the forefront of the changes in order to continue offering state-of-the-art training and education.

Students will be interested in the latest development for their future careers. Faculty will be interested as they will understand why their programs and teaching methods will need to be modified. Counseling staff will need to be updated on how to counsel students; library staff will need to know what to look for in terms of sources. Department heads, deans, and vice presidents will need to know how to adjust or, if needed, completely change the management practices of the institutions. Technological disruptions may require that creative, innovative methods be used to keep the entire institution viable and critical to student needs.

Internal Leadership

It may not be long before an institution will consider hiring a vice president to coordinate the research and reports from the research committees. It is critical for higher education leadership to understand that the digital world has the potential to completely change what is normal. It is important to remember Uber, Airbnb, and Amazon. Change will greatly impact higher education.

Changes in Program Offerings

Stage 2 impacts on higher education could result in program revisions, new programs, and deletion of existing programs. Those changes could happen rapidly. They must be foreseen and accurately predicted as the result of the research and the information gleaned should be distributed through websites, written reports, and periodic updating meetings of all concerned. Administrators, faculty, and staff must be aware of the future possibilities, willing to make changes in their work, and interested in undertaking additional training and education to meet the anticipated needs. Transparency of the research is critical to the success and viability of the higher education institution. Only proactive, future-focused, data-based decision making will keep institutions of higher education beneficial to all concerned.

CONCLUSION

Research into the development of technologies is critical to leaders of community colleges and universities who desire to be successful in keeping their respective institutions viable. Research will produce the data needed for making decisions that will affect the entire institution. This step in the process is critical for faculty, staff, administration, and most of all, students who will live in and create their careers in an ever changing, rapidly accelerating, complex world of the future.

CHAPTER 7 SUMMARY

- How does a business, health organization, economic development agency, or higher education keep up with the Stage 1 development of each of the ten twenty-first-century technologies?
- It is most easily done through research.
- It almost goes without saying that requiring community colleges to do serious, extensive research into the development of the ten technologies will not be received with immediate acceptance.
- As a result, training and re-education will be needed to help faculty and staff to understand the importance of doing research.
- The reaction of faculty and staff to the need for research, which will lead to the future success of the institution, is critical.
- Faculty need to be aware of the changes in order to revise the program; counselors will need to updated in order to properly advise students, and students will need to be aware in order to enter the workforce.
- As the technologies move from Stage 1 to Stage 2, the results of research will make certain affected programs offered at the community college to continue to be effective in an exponential era.
- University faculty and staff may find the need for research a more reasonable requirement in that the senior institutions already require significant research for their disciplines in order to move to the associate level, tenure, and full professor level.
- To begin, the institution should use the Mission/Vision Committee, which has already looked into all ten of the technologies to see which of them have the potential to impact programs of study, students, and the business community.
- Following the identification of the technologies that will impact the institution, committees will need to be set up to trace the development of specific technologies.
- In the early 1990s, software developers found that the traditional methods of planning did not work well for the development of software.
- To deal with this situation, they developed a series of steps leading toward the goal that were open ended.

- The developers worked phase by phase toward the goal, making changes to solve issues as they appeared, rather than waiting to the end.
- The software developers repeated this process phase by phase over a time period that allowed for a software to be developed that met the current needs of the business community.
- The result was that they developed a continuous, dynamic, phase-by-phase process that ultimately met the latest needs of the business community.
- The Scrum method can be used to develop a research process that is continuous, dynamic, and open ended.
- With some minor changes the Scrum process could be a valuable tool for use in higher education.
- Following the Scrum method, the committee would decide what needs to be done to reach the goal of determining where the technology is in its Stage 1 development currently, and when it is expected to move to Stage 2.
- At the end of the two-week Sprint, the entire committee meets to determine what they have accomplished so far, what additional needs have come up, and what problems need to be resolved.
- With the first Sprint completed, the committee is ready to determine the work of the next Sprint by deciding on the next objective to move toward the goal.
- One of the great advantages of this process is that it can make changes as the process goes along.
- It is critical that each committee delve as deeply as possible into the development of the technology in order to fully understand its location in Stage 1 and it potential for disruption when it obtains Stage 2.
- When the goal is reached, a report is written, sent to the Examination and Analysis Committee with a copy to the president.
- The Scrum process will help to produce more work in less time.
- If the institution has a number of research committees working on the development of two or more of the ten technologies that have potential to impact its operation and future, it will have a much better chance of keeping the institution viable.

- Each research committee should distribute its findings through the use of an internal website accessible by faculty, staff, students, and administration.
- Periodic internal meetings with the institution's leadership, faculty, and staff will become critical to keep everyone knowledgeable of when and how a specific technology is expected to impact the institution.
- It is important to remember that the business community is following the development of technologies that could help them increase production, quality, and profits.
- Further, as the technologies become available, the businesses will be looking to community colleges and universities to provide training for the workforce, management, and others on how to best utilize the technologies that apply to each of them.
- Technological disruptions may require that creative, innovative methods be used to keep the entire institution viable and critical to student needs.
- Students will be interested in the latest development for their future careers.
- Faculty will be interested as they will see that their programs and teaching methods will need to be modified.
- It is critical for higher education leadership to understand that the digital world has the potential to completely change what is normal.
- Administrators, faculty, and staff must be aware of the future possibilities, willing to make changes in their work, and interested in undertaking additional training and education to meet the anticipated needs.
- Transparency of the research is critical to the success and viability of the future higher education institution.
- Research will produce the data needed for making decisions that will affect the entire institution.

Chapter Eight

ARPAC Step 3

Planning

With research data in hand, the community college and university executives must create plans in a timely manner for the future direction of the institution. Data-driven decision making will be critical to success. As identified and corroborated by the appropriate research committee, its web information, periodic reports, and presentations, a technology that is about to move to Stage 2 should be examined and analyzed carefully.

EXAMINATION AND ANALYSIS COMMITTEE

Careful examination and analysis could be completed by the Examination and Analysis Committee (EAC) set up for that purpose. This committee should be made up of the chairs of technology committees, institutional vice presidents, and the president. This committee should do its work with all deliberative haste as the institution needs to be at the bleeding edge of understanding the shift to Stage 2 and what it will mean for the success of the institution, and its faculty, staff, and students.

Once the technology reaches Stage 2, things happen rapidly. The Examination and Analysis Committee will need to recommend how the institution should react and develop to deal with the changes the technology will make. The business community will be analyzing the technology for possible use and if it is a good fit, the businesses involved will need immediate training for its workforce. The community college and university must be prepared develop the training needed.

If the specific technology research committee involved has been doing its work of researching the development of the technology over time as it moved through Stage 1, the data the research committee brings to the table will be current. That will greatly assist the Examination and Analysis Committee in making timely decisions for the future direction of the institution.

Time is of the essence for the business community because their competitive status globally means that they must be on the front edge of the technology's benefit and be prepared to incorporate it into their processes. If the business is not ready, the chances increase for failure. If the community college and/or university is not prepared, serious problems could be created that have the potential of leading to broken partnerships with the business community.

Business/Higher Education Connections

Since the community college and university are so closely connected with the business community, higher education institutions must keep up with the Stage 2 developments as they occur. Even better, if possible, the committee researching the specific technology should be able to ascertain the future possible uses of the technology for the business community. Higher education and the business community must work hand in hand for the success of both and, more importantly, for the success of students who will become part of the workforce.

Excellent research, combined with careful analysis of the impact of the technology as it moves to Stage 2, is critical for all concerned in order to create a successful teaching, learning, and operational environment. The move on the part of the technology does not mean the work of the committee is done. Rather, it means that the committee must continue its work as Stage 2 speeds up the velocity of the technology that will create new directions for the business community, the workforce, and the higher education institution.

PLANNING: A CONTINUOUS, DYNAMIC PROCESS

The planning of the institution of higher education must become a continuous, dynamic process. It will need plans that are in line with and useful to the businesses involved. It may lead to a symbiotic relationship between the education institution and the business. That kind of relationship is not unknown in the global environment. There are businesses in the Europe that already act in this manner. Their wide use of apprenticeship programs with lengthy historical roots are one way that business and education work together for success.

Business/Education Relationships

It will become obvious to all concerned that close relationships between the business community and institutions of higher education will be critical to success of the each and, more importantly, for the students preparing for the workforce. Already there are higher education institutions in the United States as well as Europe who understand the importance of working together for the success of all concerned.

In a digital, exponential world, how does an institution of higher education operate in a successful manner for the institution, the business community, students, faculty, staff, and administration? Step 1, Awareness, and Step 2, Research, are the beginning steps of the planning process that will work successfully in the twenty-first century. Decision making based on the data collected through research is critical.

Data allows the Examination and Analysis Committee to make rapid, accurate recommendations. Those recommendations will become actual goals and objectives of the ongoing planning process. The goals and objectives must be developed in an open-ended manner in order to prepare for unanticipated new directions the technology may create for the business community. Careful planning will become a series of short-term objectives building on each other in the pursuit of the goals within the vision. The planning process must be a living document used on a daily basis.

Dynamic Planning

Since dynamic goals and objectives as the planning process is a new method, it may take some time and effort to understand and use. However, it is an adaptation that must be made on the part of higher education or it faces the possibility of withering away. Planning then is the process of deciding what needs to be done, what directions need to be pursued, where the funding is coming from, how the teaching/learning process will be developed, how the connections to business and industry will be developed, how the institution will support the community it serves, and, critically important, how the administration will lead the institution.

Planning for Success in an Exponential, Digital World

The planning process will have to become as exponential as possible. It can be done successfully with knowledgeable leaders, a faculty and staff embracing change, a student body interested in learning how to work in an ever-changing working environment, and employers who support close ties with higher education. Charles Darwin pointed out that adaptation was the key to successful development in the animal world. Adapting to a digital, exponential world is really just another step in learning in the twenty-first century in becoming successful in higher education.

CONCLUSION

The planning step in the ARPAC process is a kind of dynamic roadmap leading to goals through objectives that make success a sure thing. Adapting to the rapidly changing environment is the key to viability and success for the institution, students, the business community, the health environment, and economic development. Higher education can play a vitally important role in the success for all concerned. It will take a considerable, continuous effort, but the results are well worth the time and energy invested.

CHAPTER 8 SUMMARY

- With research data in hand, the community college and university executives must think analytically as plans are made in a timely manner for the future direction of the institution.
- Careful examination and analysis could be completed by a specific committee set up for that purpose.
- Once the technology reaches Stage 2, things happen rapidly.
- The Examination and Analysis Committee will need to recommend how the institution should react and develop to deal with the changes the technology will make.
- If the committee involved has been doing its work of researching the development of the technology over time as it moved through Stage 1, the data the research committees bring to the table will be current.
- Time is of the essence for the business community because their competitive status globally means that they must be on the front edge of the technology's benefit and be prepared to incorporate it into their processes.
- Institutions of higher education and the business community must work hand in hand for the success of both and, more importantly, for the success of students who will become part of the workforce.
- Excellent research, combined with careful analysis of the impact of the technology as it moves to Stage 2, is critical for all concerned in order to create a successful teaching, learning, and operational environment.
- The planning of the institution of higher education must become a continuous, dynamic process.
- Businesses in Europe with their wide use of apprenticeship programs are one way that business and education work together for success.

- Already there are higher education institutions in the United States as well as Europe who understand the importance of working together for the success of all concerned.
- Data allows the Examination and Analysis Committee to make rapid, accurate recommendations.
- Those recommendations will become actual objectives and goals of the ongoing planning process.
- Planning becomes a series of short-term objectives leading to a long-term goal within the vision that most likely will be metamorphosing as the process moves forward.
- The planning process will have to become as exponential and as digital as possible.
- It can be done successfully with knowledgeable leaders, a faculty and staff embracing change, a student body comfortable and interested in learning how to work in an ever-changing working environment, and employers who support close ties with higher education.
- The planning step in the process is a kind of dynamic roadmap leading to goals through objectives that make success a sure thing.
- It will take a considerable, continuous effort, but the results are well worth the time and energy invested.

Chapter Nine

ARPAC Step 4

Action

As a result of accurate research, careful analysis of data, and precise planning, leaders in institutions of higher education will be ready to take appropriate and accurate action. These actions could, for example, lead to new program development in rapid order, deletion of programs no longer needed, and rapid updating of faculty to deal with the development of the Stage 2 level technologies. Changes will most likely need to be completed in the most rapid time period possible. Year-long decision making will no longer be sufficient; decisions in weeks and months may become the norm.

GROWTH MINDSET

Leaders with a growth mindset will have the best chance of keeping up with the changes and remaining successful for all concerned. In an era of rapid technological change, serial disruptions, and continuous new education and training needs, it is critical that community colleges and universities have a method of planning that can be used remain abreast of the changes, disruptions, and needs, and ahead of the curve.

Scrum at the Department Committee Level

Take, for example, Stage 2 development of the Automotive Department. An Automotive Department Committee could set as its goal the ability for the automotive program to shift to maintenance and repair of autonomous cars. The committee would brainstorm the steps to be followed to reach to goal, such as demand for the workforce, required equipment, required space needs, faculty upgrading, program marketing, student recruitment, and the like. When that list of steps was completed, the department committee would address them one at a time in the shortest time period possible using Sprints (Sutherland & Sutherland, 2014). The committee would begin by brainstorming a set of objectives needed for the sprint. Each Sprint should take two weeks to complete.

Rather than working on the entire project, the committee members work on a specific part of it that could be completed in a couple of hours per day within a two-week time frame. Take workforce demand for example. The committee would decide what needed to be done to determine the workforce need in the district of the college. That could be done in a variety of ways from researching state and federal data to contacting local car dealers and repair organizations. The committee members would take on various parts of the project as appropriate.

Scrum Meetings

Following Scrum guidelines, the committee would meet at the end of the first week for a 10–15 minute stand-up meeting in which each member would report on the actions they had taken, what they need to address next, and what kinds of obstacles they encountered (Sutherland & Sutherland, 2014). By the end of the second week, the committee would meet, discuss progress, and what needs to be done next. The process would repeat until all the objectives were accomplished. The committee chair could write report on the findings and send them to the Examination and Analysis Committee.

CONCLUSION

Within a relatively short period of time of a month or two, the data and information would be garnered, the report developed, recommendations created, and sent on to the Examination & Analysis Committee of the institution. This may sound like a lot of work in a short period of time, but if the department and institution wants the automotive program to remain viable and successful, it is the kind of rapid work that will have to be completed.

CHAPTER 9 SUMMARY

- As a result of accurate research and scrupulous analysis of data, leaders in institutions of higher education will need to take appropriate and accurate action.
- Changes will most likely need to be completed in the fastest time period possible.
- Year-long decision making will no longer be sufficient; decisions in weeks and months may become the norm.
- It is necessary to keep in mind that when a technology reaches Stage 2, it will disseminate rapidly and widely.
- Normal change will be replaced by a change arrow that points almost straight up, which will demand rapid, accurate action on the part of the department and the institution.
- The department committee could set as its goal the ability for the program to shift to maintenance and repair of autonomous cars.
- The committee would begin by brainstorming a set of objectives needed for the Sprint. The Sprints should lead one to the next and take about two weeks to complete.
- Rather than working on the entire project, the committee members work on a specific part of it that could be completed in a couple of hours per day within a two week timeframe.
- Following Scrum guidelines, the committee would meet at the end of the first week for a 10–15 minute stand-up meeting in which each member would report on the actions they had taken, what they need to address next, and what kinds of obstacles they encountered.

- Within a relatively short period of time of two or three months, the data and information would be garnered, the report developed, recommendations created, and sent on to the Examination & Analysis Committee of the institution.
- The institutions that move rapidly and deliberately will succeed. Those that do not risk serious failure.
- The Scrum method can be used in the Action Step of ARPAC, just as it was in the Research Step.
- The department committee could set as it goal the ability for the program to shift to maintenance and repair of autonomous cars.
- The committee would begin by brainstorming a set of objectives needed for the Sprint.
- Rather than working on the entire project, the committee members work on a specific part of it that could be completed in a couple of hours per day within a two week time frame.
- By the end of the second week, the committee would meet, discuss progress, and what needs to be done next.
- The process would repeat until all the objectives were accomplished.
- Within a relatively short period of time of a month or two, the data and information would be garnered, the report developed, recommendations created, and sent on to the Examination & Analysis Committee of the institution.

Chapter Ten

ARPAC Step 5

Caring

In an exponential era, higher education leaders must care passionately about the institution. In order to make higher education institutions operate successfully in the future, they will need to be led by individuals who care deeply and sincerely about the mission and vision of the institution, its administrators, faculty, staff, students, and the various external stakeholders throughout its service area.

RESULTS OF RESEARCH

When facing serial disruptions caused by Stage 2 development of the technologies, the institution of higher education may find itself having to delete programs that may have been mainstays in the past and which have a number of full-time faculty and staff involved. If such a program needs to be deleted, the institution could decide to lay off the involved faculty and staff. At least that would have been the action taken in the twentieth century. In the twenty-first that may not be the best idea. Well-qualified faculty and staff in one area may be able to switch disciplines with some patience on the part of the institution's leadership combined with support funding for upgrading the faculty and staff.

Demand for Caring Administrators

It will take caring administrators to look for the possibilities beyond the faculty and staff's current credentials and experience. Excellent professors, teachers, and staff members are a breed unto themselves and should be provided with alternatives that would benefit them, the institution, and the students. This may be a change of thinking on the part of higher education leadership, which may have ramifications for the accrediting agencies as well, but proven educators are well worth retaining. In addition, the faculty and staff involved need to be made aware as soon as possible that changes in their status at the institution may occur.

Transparency

It is important during the ongoing, continuous planning process that meetings with college faculty and staff be held periodically at which representatives from each of the technology committees make reports on where each technology is in its Stage 1 development. This information need to be distributed transparently to all concerned in order to be of use to the institution, its faculty, staff, students, board, and other stakeholders. This will allow all concerned to see the various disruptive situations that will be faced and serve to initiate dialogues internally within the institution at all levels and externally with stakeholders.

Protection of Faculty and Staff

It must be known throughout the institution that the administration is working diligently to keep up with the technological changes it faces. Further, it must provide the unquestionable desire of the leadership that it will do everything within its power to protect its employees as the changes occur. With solid, carefully researched data, the leadership should be in a good position to understand where the institution is headed, and how it might be impacted. If that information and data is transparent to all concerned internally and externally, the prospect for a successful, viable institution can be implemented.

CONCLUSION

Caring in an ever-changing, disruptive world may seem a difficult path, but adapting is critical for survival. Caring can make that adaptation on the part of administration, faculty, staff, and students work well for all concerned. The exponential digital world is different, but it can be used to everyone's benefit if the leadership in higher education takes the time to make it work. Caring for all concerned is critical; it is also the final step in the ARPAC process that will make certain that higher education continues to serve it lofty purpose of teaching, learning, and adapting for success.

CHAPTER 10 SUMMARY

- In an exponential era, higher education leaders must care passionately about the institution, its students, faculty, and staff, the business community, and economic development agencies.
- When facing serial disruptions caused by Stage 2 development of the technologies, the institution of higher education may find itself having to delete programs that have been mainstays in the past and which have a number of full-time faculty and staff involved.
- Well-qualified faculty and staff in one area may be able to switch disciplines with some patience on the part of the leadership combined with support funding for upgrading the faculty and staff.
- Excellent professors, teachers, and staff members are a breed unto themselves and should be provided with alternatives that would benefit them and the institution.
- The faculty and staff involved need to be made aware as soon as possible that changes their status at the institution may occur.
- It is important during the ongoing, continuous planning process that meetings with college faculty and staff be held periodically at which representatives from each of the technology committees make reports on where each technology is in its Stage 1 development.
- It must be known throughout the institution that the administration is working diligently to keep up with the technological changes it faces.

- With solid, carefully researched data, the leadership should be in a good position to understand where the institution is headed, and how it might be impacted.
- Caring in an ever-changing world may seem a difficult path, but as Charles Darwin pointed out long ago, adaptation is critical for survival.
- Caring can make that adaptation on the part of administration, faculty, staff, and students work well for all concerned.
- Caring for all concerned is critical; it is also the final step in the ARPAC process that will make certain that higher education continues to serve it lofty purpose of teaching, learning, and adapting for success.

Chapter Eleven

Toward a Successful Future

Leading an institution of higher education will require leadership that is aware, caring and data-driven. The leadership must understand that planning in the twenty-first century is continuous, dynamic, and created in sequential, segmented, short-term time frames. Long-term goals will be developed in a two-to-three-year time frame within the parameters of the ten year or more vision. Short-term objectives will be developed in weeks and those objectives may be modified as they reach completion.

In addition, a number changes in short-term objectives may cause modification of the long term goals. Objectives and goals will be open ended with the understanding that as technologies develop and expand to new or unanticipated areas, planning will need to remain shoulder to shoulder with the changes. Using goals and objectives in this way develops a plan that is easily modified to meet unforeseen issues. Ultimately, it will keep the planning objectives and goals on a path to the vision of the institution.

A Dynamic Process

The direction of the institution of higher education will need to be transparent to all concerned, internally and externally, to make certain that all stakeholders understand and support the direction as it is modified. Success in this century will depend on accurate reading of all the possible impacts on the institution and appropriate action taken to keep higher education on a track that benefits the students, the business community, and the agencies of economic development. The former ivory tower will become a ground-floor dynamic engine of education and training for the benefit of all concerned.

Changing the planning method using the toboggan theory and Scrum will require a mindset founded in growth, adaptability, future-focus, and student orientation. The move to using short-term objectives that mutate while in process may be a difficult notion to understand, accept, and use; however, for the success of the institution and its many stakeholders, it is critical to do so. The ten technologies described in this book are only the beginning. Each may split off into other technologies and ideas not yet imagined will appear upon the scene.

CONCLUSION

ARPAC is a method that will allow institutions of higher education meet the needs of stakeholders internally and externally. In addition, it will allow the institutions to remain viable and successful in the twenty-first century. It will take time, effort, and exponential leadership to keep higher education on a successful track into the future.

CHAPTER 11 SUMMARY

- The institution leadership must understand that planning in the twenty-first century is continuous, dynamic, and created in sequential, segmented, short-term time frames.
- Objectives and goals will be open ended with the understanding that as technologies develop and expand to new or unanticipated areas, planning will need to remain shoulder to shoulder with the changes.
- The direction of the institution of higher education will need to be transparent to all concerned internally and externally to make certain that all stakeholders understand and support the direction as it is modified.

- The former ivory tower must become a ground-floor dynamic engine of education and training for the benefit of all concerned.
- The ten technologies used in this book are only the beginning. Each may split off into other technologies and ideas not yet imagined will appear upon the scene.
- It will take time, effort, and exponential leadership to keep higher education on a successful track into the future.

Epilogue

The intent of this book is to create a pathway for success in higher education as it faces exponential change affecting it with serial disruptions. Seven of the ten technologies—agricultural genome development, the Internet of Things, personal robots, 3D printing, autonomous cars, Bitcoin/Blockchain, and human genome development—that will impact higher education are reasonably easy to understand because their impacts are predictable to a certain degree. Stage 2 will create unforeseen issues for the institution if the technologies are not closely researched and monitored. Being caught off guard, like the taxi industry with Uber, is not where any institution of higher education wishes to find itself.

THREE ELEPHANTS IN THE ROOM

Three of the technologies, Artificial General Intelligence, quantum computing, and nanotechnology, are powerful game-changers. There is no simple way of envisioning just how each of them will impact higher education. Each could stand life and work on planet Earth on its head. Each could create phenomenal opportunities or disasters of great proportions. Community colleges and universities must be in a thoroughly researched position in order to deal successfully with each impact.

SERIAL DISRUPTIONS

As higher education wends its way through serial disruptions, some reasonable, some difficult, it will need support from research and data to make decisions that in the past were often developed by sheer guesswork and gut reaction. The next eighty years will provide many neck-jerking reactions to unbelievable phenomena. How higher education institutions deal with them is yet to be seen. Hoping others will show the way, ignoring the situation, or trying to work with it when it arrives will not be successful ways to keep the institutions intact, viable, and useful to students, the business community, and economic development. It will take well-researched data combined with careful, rapid analysis, appropriate actions, and a caring growth approach to change.

This book is an attempt to assist those in higher education to prepare for and successfully deal with the ten technologies, plus more, in future years.

Appendix

The ARPAC Planning Process: Awareness

Institutions of higher education should use committees to research which of which technologies will impact a specific community college or university.

Goal: To become knowledgeable of the ten technologies developing in the twenty-first century that could have direct impact on the institution.

Impact Committee

1. Where to start?

    - Set up a committee made up of administrators, faculty, and staff.
    - Purchase multiple copies of the books listed below, one for each committee member.
    - Assign each committee member one of the books to read and discuss the important concepts in the book.
    - Divide the books up among the committee members with an equal number reading each book.

2. Books to be read and discussed:

- Brynjolfsson, Erik and McAfee, Andrew. (2014). *The Second Machine Age: Work, Progress and Prosperity in a Time of Brilliant Technologies.* New York: W.W. Norton & Company, Inc. (ISBN: 978-0-393-23935-5).
- Friedman, Thomas. (2016). *Thank You for Being Late: An Optimist's Guide to Thriving in the Age of Accelerations.* New York: Farrar, Straus & Giroux. (ISBN: 978-0-374-27353-8).
- Kelly, Kevin. (2016). *The Inevitable: Understanding the 12 Technological Forces that will Shape Our Future.* New York: Viking. (ISBN: 978-0-525-42808-4).
- Schwab, Klaus. (2016). *The Fourth Industrial Revolution.* Geneva, Switzerland: World Economic Forum. (ISBN: 978-1-944835-00-2).
- Staat, Darrel. (2018). *Facing an Exponential Future: Technology and the Community College.* Lanham, MD: Rowman & Littlefield. (ISBN: 978-1-4758-4361-3).

3. Set a deadline of two weeks for the books to be read and ready for discussion.
4. At the discussion meeting have those who read the different books make a ten-minute presentation of the main concepts in the various books.
5. Open the committee to general discussion of the concepts.
6. Write the important concepts on a flip chart.
7. Discuss which of the technologies need to be further researched because they will directly impact the institution, local business community, and workforce.
8. When the technologies most likely to directly affect the institution are decided upon, make a list and put the report of the meeting on the internal website.
9. Assist in the development of technology committees which will conduct in-depth research into the technology and its movement to Stage 2, the exponential stage.

RESEARCH

Use a number of committees to research concerning the impact on the institution of one specific technology, such as: agricultural genome development, the Internet of Things, personal robots, quantum computing, 3D printing, artificial intelligence, autonomous cars, Bitcoin/Blockchain, human genome development, or nanotechnology.

Goal of these committees: To gain an in-depth knowledge of a specific technology expected to impact the institution in the future.

Technology Committees

1. Set up a committee made up of administrators, faculty, staff, for each of the technologies most likely to impact the institution.
2. Ask each committee to research further into the technology and its potential to impact the institution.
3. After three months, ask each committee to write a preliminary report on the findings, distribute it to administration, and post it on the institution's internal website, external website, or both.
4. At periodic meetings of the faculty and staff, ask the committee to report its findings in order to keep all internal employees aware of each committee's work.
5. Ask each committee to continue its research with the aim of determining when the technology is expected to reach Stage 2, the exponential stage.
6. When a committee researching a technology determines that Stage 2 is imminent in a matter of months, set up a new committee(s) in the department(s) that the technologies will impact to work out what changes are needed in terms of faculty, training, equipment, facilities, etc.

Departmental Committees

Goal of these committees: Determine the specifics needed to deal with the Stage 2 impact of the specific technology.

1. These committees should be made up of faculty and staff in the department(s) expected to be impacted.
2. The departmental committee(s) will research the needs for the department(s) in terms of course work, equipment, space, faculty, staff, and the like.
3. The committee(s) will present the needs to the appropriate administration members.

PLANNING

If the technology committees and the departmental committees have done their job well, the planning process comes down to the identifying the funding sources needed to deal with the impact of the technology. The process used by the technology committees could be used by other departments and divisions of the institution. If that were the case, it is a matter of finding the funding needed for those parts of the institution as well.

Goal: In order to serve the workforce and career needs of the students, the Planning Committee will need to make decisions based on the research provided by the various divisions and department within the institution.

1. The Planning Committee should be made up of the institution's executive leaders, deans, representative department chairs, representative faculty members, representative staff members, and, if appropriate, student leaders.
2. The various divisions and departments will make presentations for funding based in research that has been completed for the specific department.
3. The Planning Committee can ask questions, ask for more information, or accept the presentations as completed.
4. When all the presentations have been made, the Planning Committee will discuss and decide on which requests will be financially supported.

5. The committee will look at available funding in the normal budget process which may be able to meet the needs of some requests.
6. If additional funding is needed, the committee might decide to take certain needs to the institution's foundation for fund-raising.
7. If additional funding is available through grants, the committee might decide to pursue that route.
8. If no funding sources can be found, the committee may have to place the request on a priority for the following year.
9. Whatever process is used, the results must be transparent to all concerned internally in the institution. It is critical that faculty and staff understand why the decisions were made.
10. The entire plan for the coming year and beyond then goes to the board of the institution for approval.

ACTION

The institution takes action when the research and planning is completed.
Goal: The goal in taking action is first developing a prioritized list of what needs to be done, how to go about doing it in a rapid, dynamic manner. Any goal is made up a number of action steps, objectives that need to be worked out. The institution most likely cannot do everything simultaneously. Most likely, there will be a series of steps or phases that need to be completed in a rational order.

This is where the Scrum method can be extremely helpful. Keep in mind that the Scrum process provides a continuous, dynamic, carefully aligned method of taking action. It also allows for finding unforeseen issues that can be resolved and new positive directions that added to keep the process dynamic and thereby most useful to the institution.

Review the list below to see how the Scrum process works with a specific technology that has been identified as preparing to reach Stage 2 and will have an impact on the institution.

1. Review the existing research completed at the institution on the technology involved.
2. Decide in general what needs to be done to reach the goal.
3. Make a list of specific actions that need to be taken to reach the goal.
4. The department committee prioritizes the actions needed.
5. The department committee selects the first action step, divides the work that can be completed in two weeks (or less) among the committee members.
6. Committee members go work on their individual assignments for a two-week Sprint.
7. During the two week period, the Committee meets once or twice for a stand-up meeting, the members literally remain standing, for 10–15 minutes.
8. At the stand-up meeting(s) each committee member responds to three questions: (1) What have you accomplished since the last time the committee met? (2) What are you going to do before the next meeting? (3) What obstacles have you encountered?
9. At the end of the two-week Sprint, the committee reconvenes for a sit-down meeting to ascertain what they have accomplished so far and what needs to be done to complete the action.
10. If the action is complete, the committee is ready to take on the next prioritized action step, divide the work among the committee members and set the two-week time frame.
11. One or two stand-up meetings need to be scheduled for the committee within the two-week time frame.
12. This process repeats until all actions have been taken to meet the goal.
13. The committee then writes up a report and sends to the Examination and Analysis (E & A) Committee and the president.
14. The E & A Committee makes a recommendation to the president and the executive leadership of the institution.
15. The president can approve action to be taken, or if it is beyond the authority of the president, take it to the board for approval.

CARING

Since planning in an exponential environment requires data-driven decision making, thorough analysis, and rapid action, it is important that the administration, faculty, and staff are kept up-to-date on what is occurring. Transparency is critical, especially when serious changes in the direction of the institution are to be made. The president, vice presidents, deans, and department heads must make it clear to all the faculty and staff of the institution that administration cares about everyone and their welfare. Knowing how and when decisions are made and for what reasons needs to be transparent.

Goal: Take steps to insure that administrators, faculty, staff, and board members are fully informed as to the planning for changes in the institutions mission, vision, offerings, courses, and the like. When changes need to be made in rapid order, it is critical that the internal stakeholders are well aware of what is going on and why.

1. Hold periodic faculty and staff meetings in which the committees researching technologies can make presentations, answer questions, and lead discussion on the findings of the research.
2. Set up an internal website available to administrators, faculty, and staff that the committees researching technologies can post their findings as they go along.
3. Set up a page on the institution's external website where appropriate technology committees' findings can published.
4. As a technology approaches Stage 2, make certain that the findings of the technology committee are presented at faculty/staff meetings.
5. Transparency of committee findings will be invaluable if and when the institution has to make changes that affect program offerings, personnel changes, equipment purchases, and the like.
6. Make certain that the administration, faculty, and staff are clear about the caring for all concerned on the part of the institutional leaders.

References

Aydin, R. (2019). *How 3 guys turned renting air mattresses in their apartment into a $31 billion company, Airbnb.* https://www.businessinsider.com/how-airbnb-was-founded-a-visual-history-2016-2.

Baker, S. (2011). *Final Jeopardy: Man vs. Machine and the quest to know everything.* New York: Houghton, Mifflin, Harcourt Publishing Company.

Barfield, W. (2015). *Cyber-Humans: Our future with machines.* New York: Springer International Publishing.

Barnett, C. (2016). *3D printing.* Nottingham, England: Explaining the Future Press.

Barrat, J. (2013). *Our final invention: Artificial intelligence and the end of the human era.* New York: Thomas Dunne Books, St. Martin's Press.

Bostrom, N. (2014). *Superintelligence: Paths, dangers, strategies.* Oxford UK: Oxford University Press.

Brynjolfsson, E. & McAfee, A. (2014). *The second machine age: Work, progress, and prosperity in a time of brilliant technologies.* New York: W.W. Norton & Co.

Doudna, J. and Sternberg, S. (2017). *A crack in creation: Gene editing and the unthinkable power to control evolution.* New York: Houghton, Mifflin, Harcourt Publishing Company.

Drexler, K. (1986). *Engines of creation: The coming era of nanotechnology.* New York: Anchor Books.

Dweck, C. (2006). *Mindset, the new psychology of success: How we can learn to fulfill our potential.* New York: Ballantine Books.

Friedman, T. (2016). *Thank you for being late: An optimist's guide to thriving in the age of accelerations.* New York: Farrar, Straus and Giroux.

Isaacson, W. (2007). *Einstein: His life and universe.* New York: Simon & Schuster.

Johnson, G. (2003). *A shortcut through time.* New York: Vintage Books.

Johnson, M. & Suskewicz, J. (2020) *Lead from the future: How to turn visionary thinking into breakthrough growth.* Boston, MA: Harvard University Press.

References

Kasparov, G. (2017). *Deep thinking: Where machine intelligence ends and human creativity begins.* New York: Public Affairs.

Kelly, K. (2016). *The inevitable: Understanding the 12 technological forces that will shape out future.* New York: Viking.

Kurzweil, Ray. (2005). *The singularity is near: When humans transcend biology.* London, England: Penguin Books.

LeBlanc, R. (2019). What you should know about vertical farming. https://www.thebalancesmb.com/what-you-should-know-about-vertical-farming-4144786.

Miller, M. (2015). *The internet of things: How smart tvs, smart cars, smart homes, and smart cities are changing the world.* Indianapolis, IN: Pearson Education Inc.

O'Connell, B. (2019). History of Uber: Timeline and facts. https://www.thestreet.com/technology/history-of-uber-15028611.

Porter, J. (2019). Google may have just ushered in an era of 'Quantum Supremacy'. https://www.theverge.com/2019/9/23/20879485/google-quantum-supremacy-qubits-nasa.

Ross, A. (2016). *The industries of the future.* New York: Simon & Schuster.

Schwab, K. (2016). *The fourth industrial revolution.* Switzerland, Geneva: World Economic Forum.

Staat, D. (2019). *Exponential technologies: Higher education in an era of serial disruptions.* Lanham, MD: Rowman & Littlefield.

Staat, D. (Ed). (2018). *Facing an exponential future: Technology and the community college.* Lanham, MD: Rowman & Littlefield.

Sutherland, J. & Sutherland, J. (2014). *Scrum: The art of doing twice the work in half the time.* New York: Crown Publishing Group.

Tapscott, D. & Tapscott A. (2016). *Blockchain revolution: How the technology behind bitcoin is changing money, business and the world.* New York: Penguin Random House, LLC.

About the Author

Darrel W. Staat received his doctorate from the University of Michigan, master's degree from Western Michigan University, and bachelor's degree from Hope College. He has taught a series of eight undergraduate courses and six graduate-level courses.

He currently holds the position of coordinator and associate professor in the Higher Education Executive Leadership program at Wingate University in Wingate, North Carolina. Previously he held position of president of Eastern Maine Community College in Bangor, Maine, the founding president of York County Community College in Wells, Maine, president of Central Virginia Community College in Lynchburg, Virginia, and president of the South Carolina Technical College System in Columbia, South Carolina.

Previous publications include:
Student Focused Learning: Higher Education in an Exponential Digital Era (2020)
A Baseline of Development: Higher Education and Technology (2019)
Exponential Technologies: Higher Education in an Era of Serial Disruptions (2019)
Facing an Exponential Future: Technology and the Community College (2018)

www.ingramcontent.com/pod-product-compliance
Lightning Source LLC
Chambersburg PA
CBHW032028230426
43671CB00005B/244